The
Strength in Letting
Go

*A Journey of Pain, Healing, and
Becoming*

*He was told he was a mistake. But
what was meant to break him became
the reason he rose.*

By

Mark Chachere Jr.

For permission requests, write to:
JCsWorld1988@yahoo.com

Cover Design by Leslie Brown
Interior Formatting by Mark Anthony Chachere Jr.

ISBN: 979-8-218-78658-8

This is a work of nonfiction. Names and identifying details may have been changed to protect privacy.

Printed in the United States of America
First edition, 2025

Content Note

This memoir presents candid and authentic accounts of personal experiences, including emotional abuse, childhood neglect, addiction, grief, and trauma.

Sharing these narratives aims to promote healing and emotional well-being, not to cause harm. Kindly prioritize your emotional well-being while reading this account.

Dedication

First and always, I thank God. For carrying me through the moments I thought I wouldn't survive. You gave me strength when I had none left. For planting a purpose in my heart long before I could see it and for the grace to turn what was meant to break me into something that could build others up. To my chosen family Mike, Tiffany, Dalton, Brandon, Zach, Eva, Lora, Brett, John Boy, Maverick, Destinee, Dakota, Tom, Tommy and Jamie. You reminded me that love is not defined by blood, but by presence. You've seen me when I felt invisible yet loved me without conditions and always reminded me what family truly is. This book carries pieces of you in every chapter, because you are part of the reason I keep going and to the ones holding this book in your hand, this is for you too. For the ones who feel unseen, carried silent pain or have questioned if they were meant to be here at all. I want you to know you are not forgotten. You are not beyond hope. You are not alone. May these pages be a reminder that healing is possible, that purpose is waiting and that the very things that tried to destroy you can become the reason you rise.

With all my heart,
Mark

Preface

I never thought I would write this book. For years, I carried these memories quietly, believing they were too heavy to share and too complicated for anyone to understand. I told myself my pain wasn't important enough. Maybe if I stayed silent, it would all just fade away, but the silence didn't heal. Over time, I realized that the very things I wanted to hide were the things someone else might need to hear. This isn't a story about perfection. It's a story about survival. About learning to let go of what was breaking me so I could finally step into who I was always meant to be. It's a story about the family I lost and the family I found. About the pain that silenced me and the music that gave my voice back. About the moments that should have destroyed me but became the reason I rose. I wrote this book because I know there are others like me that've felt unseen, unheard, and unloved. Individuals who walked through darkness wondering if there was any light left at the end of it. If you're holding this book, I want you to know you're not alone. I pray these pages remind you that your story matters. That healing is possible. That purpose can grow from even the deepest wounds.

Thank you for being here with me. Thank you for letting me share my truth with you and thank you for believing, as I do, that what was meant to break you can become the very thing that builds you.

With love,
Mark Chachere Jr

Table of Contents

Chapter 1

You Weren't Supposed to Be Here

"They Said I was a mistake, but mistakes don't survive storms and I've weathered them all"

𝒯he earliest recollection of hearing such words dates to my childhood, likely between the ages of five and six. Although I was old enough to comprehend the language, I was too young to understand the reasons behind the emotional turmoil it caused. The words were uttered in hushed tones, not in the context of growth or redemption, but during heated arguments between my parents. I was always caught in the emotional crossfire, even when directed at someone else.

These words were delivered casually, as if I were an unwanted spill or an accidental occurrence. They conveyed that I had somehow entered this world in error and that my presence was never truly desired. These words became ingrained in my psyche, affecting every aspect of my life. Every Christmas morning, every school bus ride, every silent dinner, and even when I forced a smile despite my inner turmoil.

The impact extended beyond mere feelings of unlovability. It was a constant reminder that my existence was never truly wanted. I was not just the oldest; I was unplanned. Consequently, I learned to shrink, to avoid conflict, and to suppress my emotions. I mistakenly believed that survival was a substitute for being seen. This mindset made me excel at maintaining peace, even when my inner turmoil peaked. I suppressed my tears and forced laughter, even as I helped others wrap presents while my own dwindled under the Christmas tree year after year.

My goal was to become someone who could eventually be loved. However, when the individuals who created me could not accept me, I internalized their rejection. As I grew older, I wore this emotional burden as armor disguised as humility. I dated individuals who made me feel like I was too much to be loved.

In pursuit of my aspirations, I suppressed my creative pursuits, apprehensive that they might not be worth investment. I concealed songs and narratives, convinced that the world would not care if even my parents did not. However, a truth is often overlooked when someone is labeled as a "mistake": over time, the suppressed elements develop roots, and I, too, experienced this phenomenon. Despite the initial attempts to silence me, I emerged stronger and more resilient.

This narrative is not intended to accuse or evoke pity but to be released. The truth is, I was not a mistake; I was a miracle with an imperfect placement. My soul was destined for this planet, even though I was not meant to conform. I was constructed to thrive here, and my presence disrupted the cycle of fear and uncertainty. I was the light that illuminated the darkness, the breath humanity had forgotten to breathe. I recognize myself in these words not as the child who was told he should not exist, but as the man about to unveil his true purpose.

Healing does not imply that I have forgotten the past. It signifies that I have learned to navigate life's challenges without succumbing to their destructive influence. It entails the strength to reconstruct from the fragment's others deemed unworthy of preservation. It involves growing weary of carrying the shame that was never mine.

For an inordinate length of time, I believed my inability to be loved reflected my worth. I erroneously thought I would be deserving if I were more humorous, quieter, thoughtful, less emotional, or simply more of something. They would finally perceive me as a son, not a mistake, but that moment never materialized. Consequently, I took matters into my own hands.

This book, narrative, and voice are now mine and belong to everyone who has questioned their purpose in life. To every soul who has learned to apologize for simply existing, I extend this message with unwavering conviction:

You were not here by chance.
You are not broken; you are evolving.
Your presence was never excessive.

They were overwhelmed and could not cope with your brilliance. Please take the time to read this carefully and frequently.

You are not alone; you have never been alone.
Your story has not yet been told.
Until now.

It took me many years to realize that the pain I carried was not solely mine. It was generational, passed down like an unwanted heirloom from individuals who were too wounded to recognize that they were inflicting pain upon others. My parents did not invent the ache; they inherited it as well. Somewhere along the line, I became the one destined to break it. This is a solitary responsibility, as the one who possesses clarity and refuses to succumb to numbness, the one who rejects silence and acknowledges that suffering in secret is not strength. However, if I am to be the one who breaks the cycle, then I must be the one who speaks the truth. Even when it challenges the walls they constructed to survive, this book is not about assigning blame. It is about personal growth and transformation. It is not about what they failed to do; it is about the choices I made regardless.

To grow.
To rise.
To love unconditionally.

I aspire to live a whole life, even after being told I should not have existed. I must admit that this journey has been arduous.

On certain days, I still hear the echoes of the past. I still find myself attempting to shrink in spaces I can occupy. I still feel the sting of being overlooked, even in crowded environments. However, I now recognize it for what it truly is: residual. Because the child who believed he was unwanted still resides within me, but he no longer holds the reins of control.

In the present moment, I hold the pen. This chapter commenced with the falsehood that I was not supposed to be here, but it concludes with the truth: I am and am merely beginning. I now understand that the words spoken over me were never mine to keep, they reflected brokenness in others, not my deficiency. Despite the passage of years, it was challenging to separate my voice from the internal critic planted within me. I recognized that the doubt I carried had an origin, and the guilt I wore as if it was an inherited burden not a choice. The most insidious lies are those we repeat to ourselves long after the individuals who planted them have ceased to exist.

Even in silence, I could sense a subtle presence, a whisper of something more. A pull, a faint glimmer of light beneath the rubble. It manifested in fleeting moments initially: a lyric that appeared out of nowhere, a sentence that poured forth from my heart as if it had been waiting for decades to be expressed. A voice quiet yet undeniable, voiced the imperative:

"Speak the truth. It is time."

Initially, I resisted this call. I was not prepared to confront the layers of pain that lay buried. I was unwilling to acknowledge the truths I had spent a lifetime suppressing. However, healing does not occur through concealment. Eventually, my silence became oppressive and unbearable. Consequently, I embarked on a journey of writing. Not to prove anything or seek revenge. Instead, I sought to give voice to the child who once believed he lacked it. I aimed to reclaim what had been taken from me, to name the unspoken, and to begin a new with strength, clarity, and the profound realization that I had survived for a reason.

This chapter serves as my declaration: I am not mistaken. I am a messenger. A vessel for those who still carry unspoken grief. A lighthouse for those navigating storms that others cannot perceive. A mirror for those who persistently ask, "Was I ever enough?" The answer is resounding: You were. You are. You have always been. I did not write this book because I possessed all the answers. Instead, I chose to silence the voice that had patiently endured the noise of rejection, perfectionism, and fear. This voice now rises, not solely for my benefit, but for every soul who has ever questioned the significance of their story. This represents merely the beginning. A commencement founded on truth that no one else bestowed upon me, so I bestowed it upon myself. From this juncture forward, every chapter of my life will commence with this unwavering conviction:

I was always destined to be here, and so were you.

Chapter 2

The Picture My Father Had

*"Sometimes what breaks you isn't what
was said, it's what was never
acknowledged."*

$\mathcal{I}$ can still hear the things he used to say.

They weren't slips of the tongue or moments of
frustration, they were deliberate, sharpened, aimed at
me like a weapon. My father's way of speaking made
the words feel heavier than they should have been.
They didn't just land and fade away. They lodged
themselves somewhere deep inside me, repeating in
the quiet moments when no one else was around. He
told me who I would be before I could figure it out.
His "predictions" weren't about my potential or
future successes; they were insults dressed up as
prophecy. He'd say things to make sure I believed I'd
grow into someone unworthy, someone broken,
someone to be laughed at. He mocked how I talked,
how I walked, and the way I expressed myself. He
told me I'd grow up to be something shameful,
something that would make the world point and
whisper.

When you're a kid, you don't know how to
separate truth from cruelty. You take it in and believe
it. You start to see yourself through their eyes, even
if those eyes only know how to look with contempt.
It's strange, the power of words my father had, he
probably doesn't even remember half the things he
said to me, but I do. Every word, every tone, every
smirk that came after. They shaped how I saw myself
for years, and it would take me a long time to

understand that those words never reflected who I was; they were a reflection of who he was. The house always seemed louder when he was home, not in how a house feels alive, but in how tension fills every corner like a storm that hasn't broken yet. Even if the television was on or music was playing, I could hear his voice above it all. It wasn't just the words; it was how he said them. The sharp pauses. His eyes would lock onto me, like he wanted to ensure I didn't miss a syllable. His insults weren't flung casually; they were placed, like bricks being laid one by one, building something around me that I didn't know how to escape. He didn't call me by my name. He called me names. Names meant to shrink me. Names intended to make me question everything about myself before I even knew who I was. He told me I'd never be good enough and end up being nothing. Sometimes he'd twist it into mockery, predicting the person I'd become with a cruel laugh, making sure everyone in the room could hear.

I remember standing in the kitchen one evening, my hands barely big enough to wrap around a glass of water. He walked in, saw me, and smirked like my existence was inconvenient. Then the words came, "You're going to end up sucking... and be gay" (well, you get the drift on that one). I didn't respond. I didn't look up. I stared at the water in my hand, watching the surface ripple as my fingers trembled. The thing about that kind of abuse is it's invisible to everyone else. Neighbors don't see it. Teachers don't see it and even if they did, I doubt I could have explained it in a way that made them understand. There were no bruises to point to, no broken bones, only words that cut in a way you can't show anyone. Years later, I would understand that his words weren't the truth. They were a mirror of his pain, his failures, his fears, but as a child, you don't know that.

8

You think they're telling you who you are, and sometimes, it takes years to unlearn the things you were never meant to carry in the first place. I don't remember the exact day it shifted, the moment when the words stopped sinking in. It wasn't like flipping a light switch. It was more like finding a small corner of my mind I could hide in, a place he couldn't reach, no matter how loud his voice got.

I started learning the art of silence, not the kind he tried to force on me when he wanted submission, but my kind, the kind where I could hear what he said without letting it take root. I'd nod or look away, pretending the words slid right into me like they always had, but in my head, I'd quietly think, "You're wrong." It was dangerous, holding that thought. It might've lit a different fire in him if he could've heard it, but it became my secret shield. Every insult became less of a brand and more of a dull echo. Every prediction he made about my life became another thing I could prove wrong to him, and every time I passed each year and grew older, I started to see life a little differently. I didn't see it as empty anymore, as if I were waiting for spring and a new life. Waiting for the day it would grow again.

I realized that maybe I was like a tree to him. Maybe my branches looked empty to him, but something was still alive in me deep down. Something he couldn't touch, no matter how many times he tried to strip it away. I couldn't leave the house, yet I couldn't choose who I lived with or change the air I breathed, but I could select this, the silent decision that his voice would not be the one that told me who I was. That's how survival starts, not in the big escape, but in the quiet rebellion of refusing to let someone else write the ending for you. Years later, when I think back to that thought, I feel like that bare tree. I understand it in a way I couldn't as a kid. Back then, I thought I was just bereft of quality. Now I see it was a mirror of my father, because bare trees aren't dead — they're preparing. They take the storms without breaking. They survive the cold without proof of life on the surface. They hold their strength in silence until the time comes to bloom again. That was me.

Every insult my father threw, every label he tried to brand into my skin, every ugly prophecy he spoke over my life, I learned to let it hit the bark but never pierced the roots. Roots go deep, deeper than fear, deeper than shame, deep enough to hold on until the seasons change, and seasons do change. The boy, he thought, could shrink into nothing but grew quietly inwardly. Until one day, his branches spread in directions no one could have predicted, reaching for sunlight he once believed he didn't deserve. That's the thing about survival: You don't have to look strong to be strong, and you don't need anyone's permission to grow back, fuller than they ever imagined.

Looking at my life now, I realize I've been in a long, slow spring. The buds are here. The blooms are coming, and the picture my father perceived me to be? It no longer feels like a reminder of what I lacked; it's a testament to what I endured.

Chapter 3

When Santa Stopped Coming

*"The moment you stop believing in magic is the moment
of your childhood quietly dies"*

$\mathcal{G}$rowing up, Christmas was a cherished
holiday that elicited pure joy or a sense of
complexity. For my brothers and me, it commenced
with a palpable sense of reality, as we firmly believed
that Santa Claus would deliver gifts directly to our
residence during the hushed night hours. Our
unwavering faith was evident in our hushed
conversations and late-night vigilance, as we eagerly
anticipated the gentle sounds of reindeer on the roof
or the glimmer of holiday enchantment.

The house was filled with the enticing aroma of
cinnamon and pine, interspersed with the faint
remnants of last-minute wrapping paper scattered
across the floor. The Christmas tree lights flickered
softly in the darkness, casting a warm glow that, at
times, could be mistaken for mere hope. However, as
the years transpired, a gradual shift began.

One Christmas, I was confronted with the truth.
My parents revealed that they weren't the
benevolent, enigmatic figure who delivered presents
to children worldwide, but rather the embodiment of
Santa Claus themselves. This revelation shattered the

illusion of magic, causing my childhood innocence to wane and the wonder to gradually dissipate.

While I did not harbor anger towards the notion that Santa was not real, I was deeply affected by the realization that it felt was related to another secret that was not meant to be discovered. It was as if I had been privy to a deception to control my hopes and expectations.

Consequently, I assumed the role of wrapping presents for everyone else, ensuring that the paper was meticulously folded and the bows were precisely tied. I even placed gifts under the tree from "Santa," even when the packages bearing my name became smaller or, on occasion, absent.

I distinctly recall the hushed nights when I would discreetly return to the tree after everyone had retired to bed to verify the presence of gifts for myself. Occasionally, I would find a small box, while on other occasions, there would be nothing but space. I learned to accept the silence with a sense of resignation, akin to a persistent shadow that could not be dispelled.

Year after year, I witnessed my brothers and cousins eagerly unwrapping their gifts, often large, ostentatious items that elicited expressions of delight and excitement. In contrast, I carried the weight of silence, a profound sense of absence that transcended the tangible nature of gifts.

Early on, I comprehended that love could not be quantified solely by the quantity of gifts given or withheld but rather by the emotional impact of those actions. Occasionally, the most profound gift is not wrapped in paper but in the giver's presence. Last Christmas held a different significance. The presents were secondary to the simplicity of the moments shared. A candle's gentle flame, a pillow's comforting embrace, and small gestures conveyed the message of acknowledgment.

By then, I had grown weary of the superficiality, the forced smiles, and the pretense of desiring something more genuine, quiet, and authentic. I realized that those Christmas mornings were not solely about the presents. They were about the moments of being seen or unseen; sometimes, those moments carried greater emotional weight than any unwrapped gift. I offer solace to anyone who has ever felt overlooked in a room filled with love: you are more than the presents you receive. You are more than the silence that envelops you. You deserve love not only on holidays but also daily. Perhaps, true magic lies not in Santa Claus but within yourself. Even when love was absent in the ways I most yearned for, I discovered it in my voice, soul, and the unspoken promise to rewrite my story.

There exists a form of grief that does not manifest in tears. It lingers like a faint light, lingering behind the backdrop of a cherished holiday movie. Despite the laughter and festivities, one struggles to join in, a sense of detachment lingering within.

As I matured, I became adept at playing along. I would hang up stockings, light candles, and sing carols, but inside, I would search the room for something that no gift could provide: a glance, a gesture, a feeling that affirmed my worth.

The older I grew, the sharper the emptiness became. It wasn't just the stockings or the carols anymore; it was the unspoken truth that I had mastered the art of celebration without ever truly being celebrated. I smiled for pictures, I laughed at the right times, but behind those practiced expressions lingered a quiet ache. I realized that what I craved could never be purchased or forced; it was a language of love I had never been taught to read.

Every flicker of the candlelight seemed to whisper what no one else would say: that I was yearning for a place in someone's heart, a recognition that I wasn't just another face in the room, but a soul worth cherishing.

I gained a deeper understanding: love wasn't about the words spoken; it was the actions that included peace, validation, and a sense of belonging. While I may not have received these gifts during childhood, I now bestow them upon myself.

This healing process involves confronting the past that shattered me and embracing the belief that I still deserve joy, even when it eluded me in my youth.

Contrary to my previous misconceptions, healing does not entail forgetting or letting go of pain. Instead, it involves reclaiming my identity and embracing my authentic self. I remind myself that I am no longer the child who yearned for something to appear organically. I have matured into deeply rooted, thriving, and radiating warmth from within. I have crafted my self-worth with truth and am no longer awaiting external validation. Instead, I have chosen myself; perhaps this self-discovery holds the essence of the magic I sought. Consequently, when I light candles for myself it's not to conceal the silence but to honor my journey and my progress.

Even if no one taught you how to recognize your inherent worth, you are the gift this world desperately needed. There came a point where I ceased blaming myself for other individuals' emotional distress and began to unravel the underlying truths.

It was not then that I realized I didn't fail myself. It was the pervasive silence that surrounded it, the forced traditions, and the hollow laughter that failed me. People in passing with no attempt to extend that sense of belonging I yearned.

16

It was not about the gestures; it was about the lingering sense of being forgotten. As a child, I lacked the language to express this type of grief, the kind that arises not from what is taken but from what is never given. It is neither audible nor dramatic. It is quiet and persistent, lingering like tinsel, sparkling just enough to conceal the underlying weight.

Despite this, I managed to smile through it. Over time, I developed a remarkable talent for deception, mastering the art of blending seamlessly into the background. I cultivated a knack for humor, lighting candles, and showing humor that evoked positive emotions in others while harboring a secret desire to be cherished as someone's most prized possession.

However, a recurring lesson would emerge each year: when one's worth is not recognized, no amount of superficial gestures can alter the underlying reality. I persisted in earning acceptance through meticulously folded napkins and carefully selected gifts. I extended myself generously, hoping that love would eventually reciprocate. Nevertheless, when love becomes transactional, it ceases to be genuine. The more I gave in pursuit of love, the more I drained myself of energy from the individuals who failed to appreciate the value of my offerings.

Consequently, I decided to cease perpetuating the charade. Instead, I embarked on a journey of self-discovery and construction. I realized that I was never destined to remain perpetually shrinking to be invited. I was never compelled to prove my worth at someone else's table. The essence of the magic I sought, the sense of belonging, warmth, and affirmation lay not within the confines of a fireplace or beneath the branches of a tree. Instead, it was concealed beneath the layers of unspoken pain accumulated over the years, waiting for me to delve deep enough to uncover it.

With unwavering determination, I embarked on this transformative journey. I transcended the role of the silent observer and became the voice I had long yearned to express. I embodied the presence that had eluded me throughout my childhood. As I navigate through life, I no longer anticipate disappointment. Instead, I prepare for introspection. Lighting that my life requires is no longer a means of deception; it serves as a declaration of my presence, a testament to my resilience and strength. This transformation represents a miracle, a testament to the power of self-discovery and healing.

To anyone who experiences a sense of "blank space" in your life, please know that you are not alone. Your feelings are not indicative of weakness, sensitivity, or ungratefulness. Instead, you are simply an individual who requires a nurturing environment that no one else could provide. Fortunately, the healing process now rests within your grasp. You are no longer bound by the repetitive cycle of empty mornings. You are free to establish new traditions and celebrate the potential rather than dwell on the past. You've become the gift that you sought. You are the survivor of silence, the individual who chose love even in the face of indifference. You made the conscious decision to transcend the legacy of being overlooked. This chapter concludes not with bitterness, but with brilliance.
You have gained a profound understanding of your true self for this time. This realization possesses an unparalleled magic that no deception can ever diminish.

Chapter 4

Look at Jr.

"Children don't remember everything you teach them, but they never forget how you made them feel."

*I*n our backyard, there was a hole in the ground. It was a pit, where my parents had dug a hole to dispose of dead leaves and yard scraps, which they called compost. I was unfamiliar with the term "compost" then; I perceived it as an off-limits area.

They had cautioned me against playing in there, citing concerns about snakes, potential danger, and the need to avoid repetition. However, like most imaginative and curious children, I disregarded their instructions. My intention was not to disobey; I was driven by curiosity. The hole appeared to be a portal to a concealed world beneath the earth. One day, while my father was at work and my mother was home with me, I approached the pit. I recall squatting down at the edge and gently poking at the soft pile of decaying leaves, watching them disintegrate like old paper. I was engrossed in play and momentarily escaped into a state of innocence I was unaware of. Unbeknownst to me, my mother retrieved the camcorder and recorded my actions.

She stood there, filming me with laughter, zooming in on her son's dirty hands and the wonder in his eyes. She mocked me instead of offering guidance, protection, or redirecting my behavior.

The memory of her voice on that tape remains etched in my mind:

"Look at Jr. He's going to get his ass beat when his dad gets home."

In jest, she presented the video as a source of amusement, viewing my curiosity as a potential punchline for a joke. The video was not intended for archival purposes; it was not a cherished childhood memory. Instead, it served as evidence, a setup, and a warning to a child that joy and play could result in pain. When my father returned home that evening, she showed him the footage, and my mother's prediction came true. I do not recall every detail of the punishment. Still, I vividly remember the oppressive atmosphere, the palpable tension in the walls, and the intense humiliation that struck me more profoundly than any physical blow. I stood there, feeling diminutive, vulnerable, and confused, as if I were the punchline in a family that consistently laughed at my expense.

This incident was not isolated; it represented a recurring pattern of being watched rather than protected. In contrast to being reached for rather than recorded, in contrast to being shamed rather than taught, it imparted a profound lesson upon me that a child cannot fully comprehend that individuals can perceive one's actions clearly yet choose to expose them rather than provide assistance. This revelation also instilled a sense of mistrust in joy, instilling a fear that happiness would inevitably be followed by punishment and a belief that curiosity would inevitably lead to harm.

As an adult, I can still vividly recall her voice, not in the immediate vicinity, but in my memory. The teasing tone, the laughter, and the casual cruelty remain etched in my mind.

"He's going to get his ass beat."

No mother should ever find this statement humorous; no father should ever watch it and feel justified in their actions. Yet, for them, such behavior was commonplace. However, I have realized that healing from such experiences requires acknowledging and naming them, not pretending they never occurred. I confronted them directly, stating, "That was unacceptable. I deserved better."

A child deserves better treatment, and if no one else will advocate for them, I will: I extend my forgiveness to the young boy who believed his actions were his fault, thought his curiosity made him morally wrong, and felt compelled to cease exploring to survive. You no longer need to shrink or suppress your instincts. You were never the source of the problem. You were merely human in a household that lacked the knowledge and skills to provide a safe environment.

The most painful aspect was not the punishment but the betrayal. It was the realization that someone who was supposed to protect me used their voice to direct the spotlight on my shame. Over time, that moment transcended its initial status as a mere memory, becoming a blueprint for my understanding of love and my perception of what I deserved.

As a result, I ceased asking questions, wandering too far, and developed the ability to read the room, remain small, quiet, and out of trouble. If I could consistently behave to avoid being the punchline, perhaps I would not be subjected to such treatment again. However, the truth is that when the individuals around you are also broken and dysfunctional, you can be perfect, yet they will still exploit you for their gain.

Upon reflection, I recognize the profound impact of those fleeting moments on the development of my nervous system. My physical reactions, such as flinching before even approaching love, instilled in me a deep-seated skepticism towards affection. I learned to anticipate betrayal and brace myself for the potential backlash from laughter.

Raised in an environment where joy was meticulously regulated, I was constantly reminded that happiness was a finite resource, subject to the whims of the universe. Through the process of healing, I have come to realize that my upbringing in a dysfunctional environment does not limit my ability to break free from its influence. I have transcended the confines of my childhood home and no longer stand by the compost pit, contemplating the potential consequences of my curiosity, vitality, and authentic self. I have regained control of my camera, redirecting its focus inward rather than mocking or condemning. Instead, I aim to capture the essence of the young boy within the frame, conveying a message of pride:

"I am proud of you."

This pride stems from my courage to question, my ability to discover enchantment in the ordinary, and my unwavering choice to embrace vulnerability despite the ridicule I faced for expressing my emotions. To any parent reading this or contemplating the path of parenthood, I urge you to resist the temptation to capture and shame fleeting moments. Instead, immerse yourself in those experiences, impart wisdom, and honor the child's growth. Your actions today towards a child can shape the silence they carry into adulthood.

With a newfound determination, I refuse to remain silent any longer. There exists a subtle form of violence that never leaves a physical mark. It manifests in too-deep laughter, cameras that expose rather than protect, and jokes told at a child's expense, not for the sake of memory but for control. That day at the compost pit was not merely about disobedience or the presence of dirt-stained hands. It was about the moment when a child's wonder became a weapon. When curiosity, so innocent and beautiful, was weaponized for entertainment. Worse still, it was used as evidence that he deserved the consequences that followed.

I learned early that humiliation can be disguised as a smile. A parent's laughter can sometimes be louder than a shout. There is a distinction between being seen and being exposed, and when one is exposed without protection, shame becomes an inescapable shadow.

For many years, I carried the weight of a shadow that held me back. I played it safe, played small, and became adept at managing others' comfort, ensuring that I never became the reason for their discomfort. I dimmed my light until I barely recognized my reflection. However, even the faintest flame still burns. Somewhere along the way, I realized that the incident in that yard was never truly about me. It was about them, their unhealed wounds, stifled innocence, and inability to perceive wonder without controlling it. Despite bearing the burden of their reactions, I would not perpetuate their legacy.

I began to question again, not just about the world but also about myself. What would happen if I resumed playing? What if curiosity were not something to be punished, but cherished? What if the young boy in the backyard was not mistaken, but misunderstood? The answers came gradually, in fragments, in therapy sessions, lengthy journal entries, conversations with my chosen family, and the quiet whispers of a soul that never relinquished its desire to be heard.

Eventually, I did the unthinkable: I permitted myself to explore again. To make messes, laugh without flinching, and to speak without waiting for punishment. Believing that curiosity was not a flaw, but a birthright. With this newfound freedom, the shame began to dissipate. I ceased replaying the mental tape in which I was mocked. Instead, I began creating new memories, not for approval but for truth, healing, and joy.

That young boy in the dirt did not require discipline. He needed wonder reflected on him, and he needed someone to acknowledge his actions rather than criticize him. He needed someone to kneel beside him, not stand above him with a camera. He needed love. Although I cannot alter the past, I can reparent the child who endured it. I can look into those eyes and say:

"You were not wrong."
"You were not shameful."
"You were not excessive."
"You were beginning."

In honor of the children who learned to conceal their happiness, the ones who mastered the art of smiling despite shame, ones who were captured on camera when they required solace. We are reclaiming our narrative, eliminating the punchlines and replacing them with accolades. We have transcended the entertainment role and assumed the mantle of storytellers. We will continue to speak the truth until silence no longer provides a sense of security but resembles a grave.

Chapter 5
The Thing in the Culvert
"Before I knew what I was... the veil tried to show me."

$\mathcal{D}$uring my life, all occurrences of the extraordinary and the supernatural were readily dismissed as mere figments of imagination. However, my perspective has undergone a profound transformation, and I now understand that certain phenomena transcend the realm of imagination and are unveiled.

At the tender age of approximately seven or eight, I was unexpectedly dropped off at the pawn shop operated by my parents. This establishment exuded an air of roughness, resembling a building that one would pass without a second thought unless compelled to enter. Nevertheless, for me, it had a different significance. It was not merely a shop; it was where I was unceremoniously dropped, left to fend for myself, and expected to remain silent until closing time. Day after day, week after week, I was subjected to this state of supervision, neglect, and silence.

The atmosphere on that particular day was heavy, almost oppressive, exuding a sense of foreboding that clung to my skin like a miasma. I stood before the pawn shop, a place already imbued with a spiritual aura, replete with old televisions, tools that bore witness to countless stories, and guitars that once emitted melodies now hushed and silent. This establishment emanated an energy that could be perceived even by a child, yet on that day, my perception was distinct.

The culvert, situated directly in front of the store beneath the main road, resembled a dark, mouth-like opening wide and low to the ground, with concrete stretching into the inky blackness. Most children would perceive such a structure and resort to throwing stones or riding their bicycles past it, pretending it to be merely a tunnel. However, I was compelled to halt. An inexplicable force guided my actions, and my eyes were transfixed upon the culvert. A profound stillness descended upon me, devoid of fear but rather rooted in recognition; a sense of knowing that transcended comprehension. I perceived something within its depths. It defied categorization as a figure, a person, or an animal. The entity possessed a structured form but lacked a discernible shape. It emanated a presence rather than a detailed appearance. Imagine an ancient outline existing beyond the confines of time, observing me from the periphery of light. If such entities could be described, their eyes were devoid of any glow, red hue, or dramatic intensity, unlike horror movies portrayals. Instead, they were empty and vast, similar to voids that transcended my comprehension. It evoked a sense of anticipation, not in a threatening manner, but rather as a recognition of my existence. It conveyed the impression that it had been patiently waiting, not in a malevolent way, but rather as a silent acknowledgment of my presence.

When I crouched down and peered into the opening, I encountered darkness and another realm. The laws of reality seemed to converge within that pipe, revealing a spectacle beyond the mundane. Through that aperture, I did not merely observe dirt and water runoff; instead, I beheld an expansive and living entity. It defied categorization as a monster, creature, or spectral presence. It was the reality of gazing into a portal, a gateway to another dimension. It was a window into a realm that vibrated on a frequency distinct from this world, a dream that eludes memory until a sudden jolt of realization brings it all back. I witnessed colors that transcended the spectrum of this existence and a landscape that simultaneously instilled terror and holiness. It transcended the boundaries of heaven and hell, embodying a realm of incomprehensible depth. It emanated an aura of anticipation, as if it had patiently awaited my discovery.

For the first time, I experienced a profound sense of being seen. It transcended the realm of physical objects and individuals; it was a place. Paradoxically, I recognized that it was not merely external but deeply ingrained within my essence. As if the portal did not simply present me with an alternative reality, it catalyzed self-discovery, reminding me of my inherent nature. Despite this encounter's profound impact, I refrained from sharing my experience with others. How could I possibly articulate the concept of gazing into a storm drain and perceiving eternity? Yet, the memory lingers within me, a whisper, a reminder, and an anchor to a realm beyond the confines of explanation.

Standing barefoot on the gravel, my breath shallow and my heartbeat rapid, I felt an internal shift, an internal shift that was a profound awakening of my soul. This pivotal moment would resonate with me for decades, shaping my understanding of the world. I retreated slowly, never turning my back on the unseen presence, not out of fear but of a profound sense of respect.

The culvert, once a mere conduit for drainage, held far greater significance. It served as a threshold, a portal to an unknown realm. Deep within my being, I recognized an awakening, a recognition that transcended the mundane. A drainage culvert, situated outside the shop, concealed beneath a shallow slope, was half-covered in weeds. Its concrete surface, rusted stains, and shadows held no extraordinary allure, except for the inexplicable sensation I felt within its depths. Each time I passed, it lingered in my thoughts, a persistent pull, a palpable presence, and an undeniable knowing. It was as if something, or someone, was observing me from beyond the veil.

One fateful day, I encountered it once more. The nature of this entity remained elusive, transcending the boundaries of flesh and shadow. It did not instill fear within me, but rather a profound sense of stillness. Time seemed to stand still, and in that moment, I transcended the childlike vulnerability I had experienced outside the dusty pawn shop. I became a soul that had been seen, acknowledged, and understood.

Despite the profound significance of this encounter, I chose to keep it to myself, for I feared the skepticism and dismissal that would likely accompany my revelation. My parents, already attuned to my sensitivity, had labeled me as "too emotional," while my brothers, accustomed to my intense emotions, would have dismissed it as mere eccentricity. Therefore, I concealed this experience, cherishing the memory while grappling with the complexities of my unique perception.

Years passed, and I gradually gained a deeper understanding of the significance of that moment. It was not merely a peculiar occurrence, but a sacred encounter, the first attempt by an entity from beyond to establish contact. The culvert became my gateway, not a source of fear, but a catalyst for awakening.

While I am not drawn to the realm of fear, I am compelled to embrace the power of remembrance. Deep within my soul, I have always harbored a sense of difference, not superiority, but a profound connection to the ineffable. I am more sensitive, more attuned to the unspoken truths that others choose to ignore.

This inherent difference, while often met with ridicule, shame, and exclusion, also granted me access to a realm beyond the limitations of human language. As I matured, I recognized the profound impact of that moment: it marked the dawn of a new perception, a glimpse into the transcendent. Not the kind that originates from the eyes, but from the soul. And the peculiar aspect? That culvert and patch of neglected concrete gave me a clearer perception than my family ever did. In retrospect, I am left pondering: how many children perceive what adults overlook?

How many of us dismiss our earliest spiritual recollections as mere fantasies when they were introductions? Introductions to the eternal aspect of ourselves that never ceases to exist, the silent listener, the perceiver of layers, and the decipherer of messages concealed within words.

If I had confided in someone back then, they might have labeled me eccentric. However, my purpose is not to persuade anyone anymore. My objective is to remember. To honor that child version of myself who comprehended the truth. Who stood at the precipice of an unexplainable phenomenon and remained unwavering. For long before I was chosen by music or decided to share my words of truth online, I was prepared. The initial revelation did not transpire within a church setting. Instead, it occurred at a culvert, a pawn shop, on a typical Texas afternoon. In that fleeting moment, the veil lifted, uttering a single message:

"You are not alone."

Initially, I believed that the encounter by the culvert was a singular occurrence. However, the reality is that it marked the commencement of a pattern. Not merely the perception of sights, but also the profound sense of emotions and knowledge. I was not haunted by spectral entities, but rather by truths that eluded the recognition of others. As the years passed, this phenomenon persisted. I would find myself seated in a classroom, suddenly experiencing an inexplicable heaviness in the air that had no bearing on academic matters. I would enter rooms and instinctively discern the emotional distress of individuals, even without their uttering a word. I would sense aspects of people, moments, and locations, yet I lacked the linguistic means to express them and remained silent. In my upbringing, sensitivity was perceived as a vulnerability.

Intuition was dismissed as foolishness, and the unseen was attributed to the devil's machinations. Consequently, I suppressed the visions, sensations, and occasional soft voices that manifested in my dreams. I endeavored to assimilate with the mundane, but the veil never fully closed again. A culvert opened a chasm within me that refused to be sealed. On certain nights, I lay awake, eyes wide open, sensing an impending presence, not with trepidation, but with reverence. Warmth emanated from an inexplicable source, and music played in silence. I dreamt of individuals I had yet to encounter, only to recognize them years later. This gift, bestowed upon me without my request, became a burden I could not articulate.

Being chosen for a spiritual path does not solicit consent; it commences, and thereafter, life did not merely transpire; it communicated with me through synchronicities, overwhelming emotions, and prophetic pain. I do not intend to convey a mystical aura; instead, I share this revelation because I now comprehend, I was marked early. Marked by the divine, by struggle, and by a profound awareness that would eventually serve as my guiding light. While my parents documented my shortcomings and my peers ridiculed my emotions, the cosmos meticulously prepared me. Subtly, silently, and supernaturally. There is a reason the culvert found me before the church. Occasionally, God does not manifest in regal robes or deliver sermons; instead, God appears in neglected spaces, such as weeds, gravel, and forgotten corners where only the overlooked are left to await, and I was one of them.

Not forsaken but called. Therefore, when I recall that moment, I perceive not merely a child near a ditch, but a prophet in the making. I discern a messenger being summoned. I witness a boy standing on sacred ground. The entity within the culvert did not merely appear; it recognized me before I recognized myself in a world that sought to undermine everything that defied explanation. That moment is irrefutable evidence that a transcendent presence has consistently accompanied me. There watching, guiding, and patiently awaiting my recollection.

Previously, I believed that spiritual moments were exclusive to the holy, those born into peaceful households, churches, and prayer groups. However, this perception was incorrect. I discovered God in unexpected places, such as abandoned locations and moments of silence after being overlooked. Notably, the culvert became one of the initial sacred spaces I encountered. Growing up feeling invisible, the unseen became my sanctuary. I noticed subtle changes in the environment, such as the bending of light when crying, the altered movement of a breeze during emotional distress, and the impending shift in air pressure. I realized that my pain was not a barrier to the divine but an introduction to it. There were no altars, scripture, or elder laying hands on me. I was merely a child standing on gravel near a storm drain. Yet, in that moment, I felt a profound connection that surpassed any experience I had in church. As I matured, I discreetly carried this profound understanding with me.

I refrained from leading others based on this knowledge. I did not share my experiences on social media or attempt to become a spiritual guide. Honestly, I was still grappling with my understanding of spirituality. However, I came to realize that I was not mentally ill, emotionally fragile, or overly sensitive. Instead, I was attuned to the world around me. The world endeavors to numb individuals like me, to silence our feelings, our dreams, and our ability to perceive when something is amiss or beyond the veil.

Nevertheless, I chose not to suppress my heightened senses. Instead, I listened, and over time, I comprehended the gift within me, the capacity to perceive the emotions and sensations that others may not express and discern the underlying truths. This ability transcended spirituality and was a survival mechanism when the people around me failed to provide protection.

I learned to anticipate danger before it manifested. I developed the ability to discern silence as harboring potential harm. Moreover, I discovered the presence of God in even the most shadowy of places, and this culvert served as a pivotal moment, a catalyst for the veil to lift. This experience was not merely a fleeting memory but a transformative revelation that shaped my understanding of the world and my place within it.

At that moment, a voice resonated, assuring me that I was never truly alone. Upon reflection, I recognize that the culvert was observing and beckoning me. It extended beyond mere awareness, inviting me to discover my purpose.

To anyone who has ever experienced their earliest spiritual encounters as "too peculiar" to hold significance, I implore you to believe and honor them. These experiences were not mere coincidences; they were invitations. I am immensely grateful for finally embracing these invitations.

Chapter 6
The Day I Tried to Leave

*"Some of us weren't running away - we
were running toward the person we
were never allowed to be."*

The memory stands out vividly because it did
not come as a thought, a voice in my head, or a
feeling of fear. Instead, it was an entirely different
sensation. It was as if the air around me had
undergone a subtle transformation, like an activated
silent alarm, but only my spirit could perceive it. I
felt the message, not through words, but through a
frequency, a pressure in my chest and a pull in my
gut. A profound sense of knowledge that
transcended logic and demanded obedience.

The message was unequivocal: *"Leave. Now."* I did
not question it, nor could I. It was as if my spirit
guides had sounded an evacuation siren through my
bones, issuing an urgent warning. I was being
cautioned, not gently or subtly, but with an
unwavering force.

Without hesitation, I grabbed my keys and
entered the car, my hands trembling as I backed out
of the driveway. I did not pause to contemplate the
situation; I knew I had to depart. Something was
shifting, and I was not meant to remain there when it
occurred.

Some individuals may not comprehend the
nature of such a moment, which is perfectly
acceptable. For those of us who have been

unexpectedly rescued from imminent danger by an unseen force, we understand the profound impact of such an experience. It was not a figment of imagination but a form of protection, a divine interruption that compelled me to listen. In certain instances, survival demands trusting the signal that eludes the perception of others.

At the age of eighteen, high school graduation was fast approaching. Most individuals of that age occupied their minds with senior pranks, prom, or the attire they would wear when they crossed the stage. However, I was consumed by thoughts of escape and reached my breaking point. The screaming, the silence, the threats, and the name-calling, these were the relentless tormentors that assailed me. They were telling me that I was a mistake, an embarrassment, an unwanted soul who should never have been born.

Some individuals succumb quietly, while I broke with movement. I entered the car without a destination, yet I was sure I could no longer remain. I was prepared to abandon everything. The walls that had witnessed everything but remained silent. The house that claimed to be a home but never felt like one. The individuals who shared my surname could not perceive my inner turmoil, yet I never made it far. Somehow, and to this day, I cannot recall how my father discovered me. The events that transpired thereafter still resonate deeply within my being. He abruptly seized me from the car, not with words, affection, or even a question. Instead, he unleashed his fury, wielding power and striking with fists. While I do not recall every detail, I vividly remember the sound of the door swinging open, the crunch of gravel beneath my feet as I stumbled backward, and the blur of motion before darkness enveloped me. I awoke on the ground, face down in the living room.

My spirit lay in ruins, my body limp. Yet, despite the physical trauma, no one came to my aid. That moment did not merely leave me physically incapacitated; it etched a profound mark upon my soul. At the tender age of eighteen, on the cusp of freedom, I was still deemed his property to be destroyed.

I refrained from pressing charges, refrained from confiding in a teacher, and refrained from seeking solace from the school counselor. Deep within me, a conditioning had already been instilled: Disobedience brings consequences. Self-determination leads to punishment.

Despite this, months later, I still walked that graduation stage. I smiled, posed for photographs, clapped for my classmates, and waited. Perhaps they will arrive. Maybe this time, they will show up. Possibly, they would even feel a sense of pride, albeit for a fleeting moment, but they were absent. The seats remained empty, the name unspoken, and the pain concealed beneath the cap, the gown, and the forced smile.

A fragment of my younger self still resides within me, the one who attempted to save himself and possessed the courage to flee. The individual who conceived the possibility of a different life if they survived now feels indebted to that person. That day was not the day they abandoned their efforts; instead, it was the day they declared war on silence. On that day, their spirit resolved to never remain in a state of insecurity again. They vowed never to confuse blood with love and never allow fear to dictate their identity.

To anyone reading this who still bears invisible scars and recalls being punished for seeking freedom, this serves as a reminder: You were not mistaken in your desire to escape. Your courage and strength were evident, and you will eventually recognize that moment did not shatter you; instead, it redefined you. While time is often believed to be a healing force, it does not resurrect what has been buried; instead, it teaches individuals how to conceal their true selves for extended periods. Following that night, a profound transformation occurred within me, albeit subtly. It was not a dramatic or audible change; instead, it was a quiet shift, akin to the gentle closing of a door within me. I ceased sharing my feelings, harboring hopes, and reaching out to individuals who consistently demonstrated their inability to be reached. Consequently, I adopted the characteristics often associated with trauma: functional, polite, and emotionally detached. I performed the necessary actions to complete my education, smiling when expected and posing for photographs with classmates whose parents held balloons and signs in the crowd.

Upon returning home, I found myself in a place where no one had discussed the events in that driveway. There were no apologies, no expressions of concern, and no acknowledgment of my pain. It was as if my suffering had been concealed within the very fabric of my surroundings, becoming invisible, anticipated, and disregarded. That pivotal moment taught me the most perilous form of abuse is not solely physical; rather, it is the kind that instills in individuals the habit of downplaying their suffering. The kind that utters:

"It was not that severe."
"You likely deserved it."
"You provoked them into acting."

When young and uninformed, one can accept societal norms without questioning them. This can manifest in self-deception, such as saying "I'm fine" when not, or shrinking one's experiences to avoid discomfort. It can also lead to the belief that the absence of support is personal responsibility. However, upon reflection, it becomes evident that these actions were attempts to survive in an environment that was more oppressive than nurturing. Contrary to popular belief, rebellion was not a sign of weakness, but rather resilience. Disobedience was a desperate cry for freedom.

If you have ever been labeled selfish, weak, or ungrateful for leaving a toxic situation, I urge you to reconsider. Leaving is not a sign of weakness; staying in such an environment is. It took me years to recognize that I did not require anyone's permission to choose peace. My freedom did not need approval or applause; it simply needed to be pursued. While I still grieve that day, not just for the violence, but also for the silence that followed and the lack of support, I acknowledge that healing is not about denying the past. It is about accepting it, honoring the version of myself who endured it, and reclaiming my identity.

To those who left the driveway, bruised but breathing, to those who sat alone in a cap and gown, and those who still flinch when memories come too close, I want you to know that you are not broken, you are sacred. You are the proof that even silence has boundaries, and that when you distance yourself from those who harm you, you are not losing family; you are reclaiming yourself.

A profound sense of loneliness can ensue after overcoming survival challenges, distinct from the isolation of having no one. It manifests as a profound sense of unspoken experiences and the realization that no one fully comprehends the depths of one's journey. This emotional burden manifested in various aspects of my life, including relationships I overcommitted to, jobs where I settled, and conversations where I suppressed my true self to conform to societal expectations. Growing up in an environment where love could be violent, attention could be manipulative, and even freedom could be exploited, I instinctively prepared myself for potential harm, even in seemingly safe spaces and among kind individuals.

Healing from such trauma requires more than simply escaping a toxic environment. It necessitates the unlearning of the harmful lessons ingrained in that environment. Some of the most ingrained lessons I learned were:

My voice was too assertive.

My dreams were too ambitious.

My safety was negotiable.

My worth was contingent obedience
Perhaps the most challenging aspect of healing was forgiving myself for believing these falsehoods. For every time I dismissed my pain as insignificant, minimized my trauma to protect others' reputations, or succumbed to shame, convincing myself that I was the sole source of my problems, I realized that I was not alone in this journey. Neither were you.

The truth that is often unspoken is that sometimes, the most courageous act is to walk away quietly, even when no one applauds, believes, or pursues you. Becoming the person, you truly need to be is the most heroic act, even when no one has taught you how. The 18-year-old version of myself did not fail; he rose, albeit with bruises, shakes, and a sense of being broken. However, he never truly was. He established the foundation for the man I am today, a man who does not seek love but cultivates it within himself. A man who is not afraid of rejection because he has already endured the pain of being forgotten. A man who no longer requires permission to live life on his terms.

To anyone told, "You will never succeed without us," know that you will. When you do, it will not be out of spite, but out of alignment with your true self. Freedom is not about escaping your past but transcending its limitations and defining your worth on your own terms.

You have the freedom to leave, rise, and rewrite the narrative that was attempted to erase your existence, and that, my friend, is the actual graduation

Chapter 7
An Empty Seat and The Ones Who Came Anyway

"Sometimes we grieve the ones who never came... and forget to thank the ones who did."

$\mathcal{G}$raduation Day: A celebration and a glimmer of hope. Graduation day is a momentous occasion for most individuals, marking a rite of passage and recognizing their resilience. For me, it was a day tinged with celebration and a lingering sense of hope.

As I stood in the expansive hallway just beyond the stadium floor, the rhythmic footsteps on the concrete echoed through the space, accompanied by the palpable buzz of excitement and the soft squeak of folding chairs as students lined up. I adjusted my cap and gown, my heart pounding in my chest, not out of apprehension for the ceremony, but out of a deep-seated hope that had not yet dissipated. Perhaps my parents would attend, walking through those stadium doors and taking seats in the audience. Maybe they would appear even after the challenges and hardships I had endured, including the conflicts, silence, and pain. However, I was aware of the likelihood of their absence, a realization that had been etched into my mind long before this day.

When my name was finally called, I stepped onto the stage, but instead of the silence I had anticipated, I was greeted by the presence of my

Aunt Patty and a few close friends. These individuals, who were not related by blood but had shown unwavering support for my heart, clapped, smiled, and made eye contact in a room where I yearned for recognition. Their presence filled me with gratitude and a profound sense of appreciation.

Despite the overwhelming joy and gratitude, I could not suppress a lingering search for my parents. Even as I heard my name echoing through the stadium, I scanned the crowd, hoping to glimpse their faces. I envisioned them arriving late, quietly taking seats just in time to witness my triumph. However, this dream remained unfulfilled, and the absence of my parents became a poignant reminder of unfulfilled expectations.

It is possible to experience both deep gratitude and profound grief simultaneously. One can be thankful for those who attended while yearning for those who did not. This complex emotional landscape represents the essence of healing. It is not a straightforward process but a journey that encompasses beauty and disappointment, honor and heartbreak. After the ceremony, I took photographs, smiled, and embraced those who truly cared for me. In celebration of my graduation, I gathered with my family, the individuals who consistently demonstrated unconditional love and support, never making me feel the need to earn their affection. Later that evening, in the quiet moments, I shed tears, despite the triumph and joyous occasion. Even as I stood on stage, basking in the cheers and surrounded by love, a profound sense of loss lingered. My parents' absence weighed heavily on my heart, not because of gifts or grand celebrations but because of their profound absence. It was not about the tangible expressions of love but the sacred act of someone being there, witnessing my journey, and affirming my worth.

Reflecting on this momentous occasion, I realize their absence did not diminish my value. Instead, it unveiled their limitations, revealing their capabilities and shortcomings. It exposed the path I never desired to follow. In truth, I will consciously try to be present for the individuals I love, even those who may be overlooked or forgotten by society. I will honor the child within me, whispering, "Please do not abandon me."

This chapter, this memory, and this day have transcended my parents' absence. They are no longer the defining factor but merely a chapter in my life's story. I extend my heartfelt gratitude to Aunt Patty for being a constant presence in my life. To my friends who stood in the gap during my absence, I acknowledge your unwavering support. To anyone who has quietly shown up for me, without seeking recognition, you are an integral part of my survival narrative.

To the reader, I empathize with the pain of unfulfilled expectations. If no one attended your momentous occasion, I offer my condolences. If only one person did, I urge you to express your gratitude with every opportunity. Sometimes, the quietest presence can make the most profound impact. A lingering ache persists after milestones, not from the tangible gains, but from the unacknowledged absence. Society often emphasizes pride, holding one's head high, and celebrating accomplishments as a badge of honor. However, it fails to prepare us for the echo of absence. Even in a room filled with cheers, our hearts may still yearn for the presence of those who are missing. Even with our diplomas, a sense of incompleteness can linger, reminding us of the individuals not there to witness our triumph.

Over the years, I endeavored to convince myself that the absence of my parents' presence at my graduation ceremony was inconsequential. I rationalized that love was not contingent upon grand gestures or stadium applause. However, the truth is that, even at the tender age of eighteen, a child yearns for their parents to acknowledge their presence, express pride, and affirm their accomplishments. Regrettably, I failed to receive this validation. For an extended period, I carried shame because I still desired it. I erroneously believed that healing entailed ceasing to crave it. Healing entails ceasing to define oneself by its absence. Despite their absence, I rose to the occasion. Despite their indifference, I persevered. Despite their missing opportunity, I remained steadfast in my purpose.

While they could not attend, Aunt Patty demonstrated her unwavering support with her whole heart. My friends arrived with unbridled joy and pride. Even strangers in the crowd became witnesses I had never anticipated but will forever cherish. Their presence, though unexpected, was a testament to the power of chosen and intentional love, which can surpass even familial ties.

I extend my acknowledgment to anyone who stood in the hallway, robe billowing, heart pounding, fervently praying for someone to enter. I empathize with those who walked that stage with a smile concealing a profound sense of loss. If you have ever scanned the crowd, even now, for the individuals who failed to attend, know that your desire for their presence does not render you broken. Your absence does not constitute weakness but signifies your unwavering determination to persevere. Showing up for yourself when no one else does is the foundation of a legacy that cannot be erased.

I had finally achieved a respite. I was residing with a coworker, who generously offered me a couch, a respite, and a fleeting moment of tranquility I had not experienced in years. While the circumstances were not glamorous, they were mine. They were quiet and secure and allowed me to breathe without the constant need to tiptoe.

I had meticulously planned an intimate gathering for weeks, a simple yet profound moment of connection and presence. I had clarified that gifts and praise were not my desires; instead, I yearned for genuine human interaction. I sought proof that my worth extended beyond obligation, that someone would try to show up when they could have easily avoided it.

In the days leading up to the event, I performed a meticulous cleaning routine, transforming my home into a welcoming space. I rearranged the furniture, polished the windows, and ensured every light functioned properly. I procured an ample food supply to accommodate double the number of guests who had indicated their attendance. While I contemplated wearing something new, I ultimately chose an outfit reflecting my authentic self.

As the time drew near, unease began to creep in. I constantly checked my phone, watching the digital numbers slowly accumulate, mirroring the passage of time. Unfortunately, many of the individuals who had promised to attend failed to respond or even leave me on read. One even posted online at a completely unrelated event that same evening. This realization was harrowing, underscoring that they prioritized other commitments over my gathering.

I lingered by the front door for an extended period, my gaze fixed on the empty chairs I had meticulously arranged, symbolizing my hopes and expectations. One chair was reserved for her, another for him, and a third for the friend who had assured me of their presence. Regrettably, they had all missed the event.

The most challenging aspect of this situation was maintaining a composed demeanor and playing the role of a gracious host. I had to feign happiness and pretend I was not slowly succumbing to the weight of my own emotions. However, amidst the facade of composure, there was a glimmer of hope: the presence of those who had made it.

Although they may not have arrived perfectly dressed, punctually, or adorned with balloons or cards, their tangible presence was what truly mattered. Suddenly, I ceased counting the empty chairs and stopped obsessing over the absence of those who had not shown up. Because the individuals who had attended saw me, they had chosen me. Not because they felt obligated to do so, but because they genuinely wanted to.

That evening, I imparted knowledge that surpassed the counsel of any therapist. I realized that I had squandered countless years attempting to garner support. I had endeavored to persuade individuals to care for and nurture lifeless plants with the fervent hope that they would revive. However, it is important to recognize that attendance is unpredictable, and it is unreasonable to expect constant begging.

Following that night, a profound shift occurred within me. I resolutely decided to cease pursuing those lacking interest or motivation. I refrained from pleading with individuals to acknowledge my presence. Instead, I prioritize having a single individual with genuine compassion over many indifferent individuals. That transformative evening profoundly altered my perspective on life. When I embark on a plan or open my heart, I no longer await their arrival with apprehension. Instead, I focus on the individuals who choose to participate, and it is from this gathering that the narrative truly commences.

Chapter 8
The Whisper Beneath the Wreckage
*"Some of us were cracked open so
something holy could find its way in."*

$\mathcal{I}$ndividuals frequently inquire about the moment I discovered my unique gift. Some refer to it as a "sixth sense" or an "ability to perceive and comprehend things beyond the notice of others." However, I did not experience a dramatic revelation or encounter a supernatural entity. My gift manifested subtly, beginning with faint whispers and subtle nudges that felt as if they were not my own. I could sense impending phone calls before they rang and even feel the grief of others as if it were my own, even when they were smiling. Initially, I attributed these abilities to being "too sensitive."

This was a common refrain, often accompanied by the labels of "too soft," "too emotional," and "too much." However, there was one crucial aspect that no one had informed me: sensitivity is not a flaw but a spiritual frequency. It is not deficiency; it is a signal.

Over time, the subtle whispers grew louder, not in volume, but in clarity. I began to perceive things within the silence. I would dream of events that subsequently transpired and enter a room and sense the arguments that had already occurred. I was initially overwhelmed and convinced that I was losing my mind.

Nevertheless, this does not adequately explain the instances when I would write down a message for someone, only to have them react with shock and disbelief because it was something their mother had said to them before passing away. This does not explain why I could sense the pain that individuals had kept silent for years or why strangers felt comfortable sharing their life stories with me without any apparent reason. This was not madness; it was awakening. I did not request these abilities; they simply manifested within me. I did not pursue them; they arrived. They found me, as if the gift had been patiently awaiting my readiness. Alternatively, perhaps the pain I endured, including physical, emotional, and spiritual abandonment, left me attuned to subtleties that others overlooked. I recall a period in my life when I escaped from these challenges, finding solace in physical, emotional, and spiritual distance from my family and comfort. However, I was surrounded by space for breathing while cohabitating with a coworker, a space for listening, and in that stillness, something began to awaken within me.

I started to perceive the unspoken, notice the subtle energies emanating from individuals as they entered a room, and eventually, I realized that my existence extended beyond mere survival. I was here to transmit. There were moments when I resisted this awakening, dismissing it as mere imagination, attributing it to coincidence, or my emotional state and projection of my wounds onto the world. However, the messages persisted.

A friend's grandmother, who had passed away, would suddenly hear her favorite song playing at the precise moment when her friend needed comfort. I would wake up with someone's name in my mind and send them a message, only to discover that they had recently lost someone or were seeking solace in prayer. On one occasion, I placed my hand over someone's heart and simply said, "It's okay now." They responded with tears, revealing that I had spoken words that their mother had whispered during hospice.

These experiences were not mere figments of my imagination. They were undeniable truths. This was not a matter of delusion. This was a calling, and it took me many years to acknowledge it without hesitation: I am a vessel. A receiver. A communicator. A channel for the inexpressible words of the living and the unspoken messages of the departed.

What is truly remarkable is the convergence of music and spirit. The lyrics that came to me felt guided, and the melodies emanated from a source beyond my ego. Songs transcended their conventional role as mere music; they became messages. At times, I find myself in a peculiar state, bridging the gap between trauma and transformation, the earthly realm and the divine. During this transformative journey, I contemplated the possibility that healing may not be my primary purpose. Instead, I realized that my role might be to assist others in their healing process. Recognizing my imperfections, I understood that I had shed every wound to become a source of support for those seeking solace. While I may not possess all the answers, I embrace the simplicity of confronting every painful question that led me to this profound realization.

On certain days, I find myself asking, "Why me?" Why was I entrusted with this unique gift? Why was I burdened with these peculiar messages, visions, dreams, and emotions? The answers, though subtle, come to me with clarity each time:

"Because you listen."

"Because you retain memories."

"Because you were willing to confront the darkness and stand firm when the light arrived."

I did not grow up with the term's "empath" or "intuitive." I recognized my heightened sensitivity in a world that sought to diminish it. When emotions were labeled as weaknesses, I instinctively concealed my gifts. Spiritual gifts, however, do not perish in hiding; they endure, patiently awaiting their opportunity to manifest. I now comprehend that my sensitivity extended beyond mere emotions; it served as an antenna, attuned to grief, joy, and narratives that did not belong to me yet somehow passed through me on their journey to another.

One night, while lying in bed, eyes wide open and body still, I heard a woman whisper a name I did not recognize. The following day, a friend mentioned the same name in passing, revealing that it belonged to her grandmother, who had passed away many years ago. I refrained from disclosing what I had heard at that time, as I still harbored doubts about my evolving abilities. However, I now recognize that my intuition was not a figment of imagination. It was a recollection, a glimpse into something my soul already knew. I arrived on this earth with more than pain and a purpose.

Unfortunately, there is a lack of discourse surrounding the wreckage that gives birth to a calling. People yearn for the light, the wisdom, but they fail to acknowledge the transformative process that precedes it. The Miracles! However, what about loneliness, or even the confusion of hearing things that no one else perceives? What about the silence when you speak a truth that the room is unprepared to receive?

For an extended period, I grappled with this challenge. I yearned to silence it, to conform to societal norms. However, whenever I attempted to suppress it, it intensified, not to torment me, but to awaken me. This gift has never demanded perfection; it has simply requested my presence. It has compelled me to sit in the presence of others without flinching, to listen beneath the cacophony, to feel beneath the words, and to sing what others are afraid to express.

Occasionally, the message is not conveyed through the lyrics; it lies in the vibration, the silence between the notes, and the fleeting moment when someone experiences a song and rediscovers a forgotten aspect of their essence. For me, music has become a path back to the soul. When I sing, I recognize that my voice is not solely my own. It encompasses the echoes of my ancestors, the forgotten children, and the individuals who never could express themselves through me, ensuring their voices would not be silenced. This phase of my life is no longer about proving anything; it is about honoring the gifts I possess. Trust that if the Divine bestowed upon me this frequency, it was with the intention of allowing me to resonate with it, not to suppress it. Therefore, if you have ever experienced a profound sense of pain that catalyzed personal growth, or if you have felt like your emotions were excessive, I want you to know: You are not flawed. You serve as a bridge between pain and healing, between the past and the future, between our world and the realm of remembrance.

Chapter 9

When Love Made Them Leave

*"I didn't lose my family because I
married a man. I lost them because they
were never willing to love me as I was."*

*U*nbeknownst to me, choosing love entailed
the potential loss of theirs. It was not an abrupt
severance; instead, it was a gradual process. It was
almost like I was attempting to maintain a phone line
that perpetually experienced interruptions until
silence became the ultimate solution one day. I
would peruse my contacts, momentarily pausing at
their names, my finger hovering over the call button
as if it were an incantation for resurrection.
Ironically, one cannot resurrect what was never truly
alive. Contrary to popular belief, rejection can
manifest in subtle and unsettling ways. It does not
occur in dramatic explosions, slammed doors,
screaming matches, or ultimatums. Instead, some
rejections are more insidious, happening gradually
and without fanfare.

This was the case when I entered marriage. I
harbored a glimmer of hope that my family would
finally perceive and support me by constructing a
sacred and deeply rooted bond of love. Perhaps love
would bridge the gap between my true self and the
persona they had always envisioned for me.
However, this was not the case.

The silence descended upon me swiftly, not because of a quarrel or a falling out. It was simply the absence of communication. Calls went unanswered, text messages remained unread, and invitations were disregarded. When I finally received a response from my mother, I will never forget the words she uttered:

"I simply do not find him agreeable."

She was referring to my husband, who had never raised his voice to her. He had made an earnest attempt to connect, albeit awkwardly, and had consistently strived to be accepted. She had never expressed disapproval of my homosexuality, and I did not require her to do so. I had already realized they had established preconceived notions about who I could be. The moment I transcended these boundaries, they did not merely disapprove and vanish, even in the embrace of love and commitment. That aspect of the experience was the most profound and painful moment. Not merely disapproval, the judgment, but abandonment.

In that moment, I became a mature individual who had discovered someone to share life with, regardless of the consequences. The individuals who should have been proud of me for finding love responded as if I had passed away. Despite being married, I was in a state of mourning, not for the marriage itself, but for the relationship I never truly had with my parents. I yearned for them to accept me unconditionally.

I repeatedly contemplated:

"If they could only perceive the love we shared…"

"If they could only gain an understanding of him…"

"If they could only soften their hearts…"

However, their silence persisted.

The distance between us grew longer each day, and I gained new insights. I discovered their love had conditions, and I had inadvertently crossed the threshold that caused those conditions to collapse. They no longer controlled me, nor could they mold me into a conformist, safe, and diminutive individual. They could no longer ignore my true self. Consequently, they chose to distance themselves from me.

It is essential to clarify that my ex-husband was not without flaws, and neither was I. Our marriage ultimately failed. We both engaged in actions that caused pain to each other. Neither of us deserved their cruelty, nor did I. Regardless of the outcome of our relationship, it originated from a foundation of hope, honesty, and self-acceptance. It marked one of the first instances when I consciously prioritized myself without apology, concealment, or compromise. They punished me for this act of self-assertion. In retrospect, their silence taught me the true nature of love. Real love does not falter when it encounters disagreement. It embraces it, it engages in dialogue, creates space for understanding, and remains steadfast.

When it causes pain, genuine love provides healing; it does not abandon. Ironically, their absence gave me a gift: the freedom to cease seeking their approval. The courage to become the man I was always destined to be. The space to comprehend that unconditional love is not love at all. Therefore, if you have experienced the loss of individuals due to your pursuit of yourself, your truth, your identity, your partner, and your peace, I want you to know that this was not a loss. It was a revelation, a shedding of false love. A graduation from surviving on scraps. You did not lose your family; you merely lost the illusion of it.

You construct it with individuals who do not recoil from your light.

I once believed they would eventually reciprocate my kindness, quietness, and forgiveness. I endeavored to serve as a bridge, shrinking myself to make them comfortable crossing. However, you can only fold yourself so many times before something fractures, and for me, it finally did. As I matured, I realized I would never be genuinely invited in. Not truly. Unless I played a role that was not my own, they did not desire my wholeness; they desired my obedience.

They sought the version of me they could readily explain to their acquaintances nearby, the version that did not make things "difficult, " the version that refrained from expressing my love openly. I must share this truth: love that cannot breathe in public is not love. It is a regrettable facade disguised as tradition.

For many years, I carried the weight of blame, convinced that I was the one who had failed. If I had merely handled matters differently, softened the truth, and diminished the aspects of myself that frightened them, perhaps they would still be present. However, I now perceive the situation with clarity: I did not lose my family. They were the ones who chose to depart. They decided to walk away the moment I decided to embrace the truth. What they will never utter aloud, but what I now deeply comprehend within my core, is this: my love confronted their limitations; not because I imposed anything upon them, or me exhibiting aggression, defiance, or anger. It was because I existed in full view. For individuals who cannot confront their reflections, visibility feels like violence, and it will gnaw at you relentlessly.

You may not fully comprehend the weight of false love until you release it. When I finally decided to let go, I ceased begging for calls, explaining myself, and reaching across vast distances for silence, and an unexpected transformation occurred. I discovered a sense of peace, albeit not immediately or without grief. It was a genuine, grounded peace that did not rely on someone addressing me as "son" to validate my worth. It allowed me to construct a sanctuary without seeking permission to feel safe.

To anyone reading this who has experienced the grief of losing living loved ones, I empathize with your pain. It is a unique form of heartbreak, mourning the presence of someone while they are still alive, laughing, living, and sharing family photos that you will never be a part of. However, I urge you to listen closely: You are not abandoned. You are being redirected away from places where your spirit was never secure and towards individuals who can truly see and support you. I assure you that when you cease pursuing those who have abandoned you, you will finally create space for those who can meet you on a deeper level. Do so entirely, freely, and without hesitation.

Chapter 10

The Deployment Surprise

*"I came home from war expecting a welcome.
Instead, I met silence in aisle
nine."*

$\mathcal{U}$pon returning home from a deployment, one would expect to be greeted with the utmost reverence and love. However, my experience was far from that. My parents' response was unexpected and disappointing despite my service and sacrifices. I did not wear my uniform or make grand gestures upon my return. Instead, I approached the situation with humility and quietness, seeking solace in the presence of my cousin and aunt, who had consistently shown me unconditional support. We planned to surprise my parents by visiting Walmart, an hour and a half away. We had no prior knowledge of their whereabouts and hoped that this unexpected gesture might foster a moment of healing and reconciliation. However, our efforts were met with silence and indifference. My parents had seemingly vanished without a trace. They were not found in the store, at the checkout counter, or even in the parking lot. Instead, they had chosen to leave me alone, their absence leaving an indelible mark on my heart.

I attempted to reach out to them through phone calls and text messages, but my efforts were met with irresponsiveness. Finally, one of them answered the phone, but their voice was cold and measured, as if I was an impersonal work call rather than the voice of a son they had not seen in months. They did not explain their absence, made no apology for their actions, and stated that they had gone to a nearby restaurant.

Undeterred, we drove to the restaurant, hoping to find some semblance of connection. The establishment's public nature, with its bright lights, clinking plates, and booths that fostered awkward silences, provided an ideal setting for a reunion. However, my hopes were dashed once again. My parents remained seated, their faces expressionless and indifferent. They did not rise to greet me, reach out to embrace me, or even acknowledge my presence. Instead, they continued to dine in silence, their absence a stark reminder of the emotional distance that had grown between us.

I felt like an outsider in their presence, a stranger they had not thought of in weeks, perhaps even months. Their reaction was one of detachment, as if I were not their blood returning from a deployment. It was not because I was out of place; instead, it was the simple fact that I was unwanted.

I remained silent, tearful, and composed. However, inside, a profound sense of loss was shattered. It was not rejection that had caused this emotional turmoil; instead, I had inadvertently severed the bonds of their love by simply being myself.

That dinner was brief, awkward, and devoid of warmth. The details of what I ordered or what they said elude my memory, but the weight of unspoken words lingered heavily. They failed to inquire about my well-being, experiences, or perspective during my absence. In essence, they no longer saw me.

That evening, I left with a profound realization that it would take years to comprehend fully: some individuals will never celebrate your return because your growth challenges their control. In some cases, the individuals who gave birth to you will grieve for the person they envisioned you to be rather than celebrate the individual you have become.

It was not until much later that I began the arduous journey of healing. As I retrospectively examined that day, I realized it was not the moment I lost them. I had lost them long before that. That day merely served as confirmation of a truth that had been simmering for some time. The funeral, which I had clung to as a fantasy, was a futile attempt to appease their unwavering disdain. Where they withheld love, I began receiving it from unexpected sources, from strangers, music, and within myself. In its infinite wisdom, the Divine affirmed the truth they had denied. Where they had withheld love, I found solace and acceptance from the very essence of existence.

To anyone who has returned home from a journey, a deployment, a relationship, or a period of pain, only to be met with cold stares instead of open arms, I want you to know that you are not alone. You are not too much, and you deserve a celebration. You deserve presence, and you deserve love that acknowledges your return. If you did not receive the support you sought from those you believed would provide it, you will find it from those destined to hold your arrival in high regard.

Previously, I held the belief that survival fostered loyalty. If one endured a challenging experience, surpassing their limitations, and emerged victorious, the individuals who professed their love would extend their embrace upon their return. However, my understanding has evolved since that fateful evening at the restaurant. I have realized that some individuals fear your awakening, rather than your demise. Awakening signifies a shift in perception, leading you to recognize them for who they truly are. Once this realization dawns upon you, you cease seeking their approval.

That dinner was not merely awkward; it was calculated, an observance of a scene from a play where each participant is fully aware of their role, yet I remained oblivious. Their demeanor was cold and distant, and their responses were measured and calculated. Their attention was diverted towards their side dishes rather than my survival. This was not a lack of knowledge regarding my recent ordeal; instead, they were unable to control the version of myself that emerged. I did not seek permission or validation; I returned whole, or at least, on the path to wholeness. This realization posed a threat to them, as individuals who cannot manipulate your identity or instill guilt to diminish your self-esteem. It tends to convince them that your distance is a sign of your liberation.

That evening, a profound transformation occurred, not instantly, but gradually, as if a quiet door creaked open within my chest. I realized that I had been persistently demonstrating my worthiness, while they had been subtly asserting their disinterest. I continued to offer my heart, assuming that it was still subject to debate, but it was no longer.

Exiting that restaurant, I experienced a profound sense of clarity, devoid of anger or sadness. It was as if a veil had been lifted, revealing a new perspective: they had not rejected me; they had never held me to their expectations. Consequently, I ceased attempting to maintain contact, refrained from monitoring their responses, and ceased accommodating individuals who consistently disregarded my boundaries. Although this decision may be emotionally challenging, it has proven to be one of my most liberating actions. Healing does not always manifest as closure; it sometimes feels like detachment. It entails finally allowing the version of myself that sought their approval to find peace.

To anyone who has entered a room, yearning for recognition, only to be met with silence, it is essential to recognize that you did not demand an excessive amount. You sought validation from the wrong individuals. Your presence is sacred, and your return is revered. The universe celebrated your return, even if they could not celebrate your achievements. The moment you emerged stronger, the divine applauded, and I joined in their celebration.

They were unaware of the nightmares that haunted me or the incessant, empty silences that followed the chaos. They were unaware of the emotional toll of navigating the chow hall, knowing whether to address specific issues, or the lingering impact of being 7,000 miles away and still feeling the weight of home pressing upon me. They did not inquire, and perhaps they did not wish to. However, it is crucial to acknowledge that the version of myself who departed was already uncomfortable for them. Consequently, the version of myself who returned, fully awakened and vulnerable, was too much for them to handle.

Chapter 11

Eulogies for Connections That No Longer Live

"Sometimes the quietest moments scream the loudest truth."

$\mathcal{I}$n retrospect, I failed to recognize that the table served not only as the site of an uncomfortable reunion but also as an altar. My demise that day was not my aspiration; it was my delusion. I shattered the illusion that they would ever be capable of loving me as I required. The meal shared that day was not a celebration but a mournful repast. I quietly grieved amidst the clinking of silverware and the emptiness of their stares. When I reflected in the window adjacent to our table, I failed to recognize anyone seated there. It was not because I had undergone a physical transformation, but rather because I was finally beginning to perceive myself without their distorted perception. There was no toast, no warmth, only the gradual and excruciating pain of feigning normalcy when the depths of my soul were in turmoil. I responded appropriately at the designated moments, smiled when it was expected, and nodded when silence was appropriate. I observed the performance unfold, each of us playing our roles as strangers in a scene that had never been rehearsed. I was the sole individual who comprehended that the curtain had already descended.

They discussed mundane topics such as work, traffic, and weather, avoiding mentioning what truly mattered. No inquiry arose regarding my transformation, experiences, or the profound sense of disorientation I experienced upon returning from war to a place that no longer felt like home.

Somewhere between the appetizer and the bill, I ceased to anticipate their attention and, deep within my being, I uttered a hushed farewell not to them but to the version of myself that persistently clung to the hope of a miracle that would never materialize. That chapter has concluded, not with animosity or malice, but with a profound sense of peace, a peace that arises when one ceases to expend energy on sustaining something that is already beyond repair.

There are funerals we never attend. Not because we were not invited, but because the death was quiet, emotional, and unspoken. I never stood over a casket to mourn this relationship. There were no flowers, whispered prayers, or a moment of silence. Make no mistake, something died. It was not a sudden passing, but the death that unfolds slowly over years, like a light dimming in a room where no one notices until it is pitch black. You were already gone when I realized how dark it had become. Not physically. You still exist. Still breathing. Still post photos of smiles that don't reach the eyes. The part of you that once met me in the middle? That part no longer resides here, and I grieved quietly. In the corners of conversations that once felt safe. In the silent scroll through old memories, trying to find the frame where it all went blurry. There were so many versions of you that I loved. The one who laughed without calculation. The one who protected me like fragile glass. The one who showed up when no one else did. Over time, those versions faded. I kept trying to resurrect them with patience, grace, and silence, until silence became its kind of burial ground.

I composed eulogies in my mind for months, drafts I never spoke aloud. How do you tell the world you're grieving someone who still texts "Happy Birthday"? Who still shows up at Christmas with a smile but leaves their soul at home?

This chapter is not about bitterness. It is not an accusation. It is a farewell to the illusion that we were still what we once were. I cannot continue to grieve a ghost while pretending we are alive.

So here it is:

My goodbye to the idea of us.
My final bow to the role I
played in a story
that no longer bears my
name in the credits.
May peace finds us both,
even if it's in separate
places.
May you live fully in the
world you chose.
May I finally cease
bleeding for a bond
that no longer breathes.

It is a strange kind of mourning, grieving the living. The absence of rituals, such as receptions with soft music, lukewarm coffee, and gentle condolences from those who once comprehended the depth of our connection, left me with a profound sense of silence. I found myself seated across from someone whose eyes once held recognition, now reflecting through me as if the shared years were mere scenes from a forgotten play. With no outward indication of departure, I withdrew into solitude, acknowledging that attempting to revive a withering plant was futile. My efforts were merely delaying the inevitable acceptance of its demise.

I had expended all my efforts to maintain a connection that no longer resonated with me. I had replayed old memories, seeking solace in their purported proof of a sacred presence beneath the silence. I had molded my spirit to conform to a frame that no longer belonged to me. Some relationships do not conclude with explosive conflicts; they dissipate gradually.

Initially, the absence was subtle, a missed call here, a brief reply there. Gradually, the distance between us widened, and my words felt like echoes. I gazed at my reflection, contemplating how long I had been the sole one reaching across the table. With reverence, I released myself from that relationship. What we shared once held significance, shaping me, causing pain, imparting wisdom, and breaking me. However, that version of us belonged to a past that no longer exists. Attempting to resurrect it would only dishonor the healing journey I had undertaken.

I no longer seek the approval of those who have forgotten my essence. I no longer crave applause from an audience that departed the theater years ago. I no longer feel compelled to perform a role that has outgrown me.

Unlike the one I had envisioned, this conclusion was the one I needed: quiet, pure, and complete. I extend my gratitude to the spirits still seated at tables we no longer share. For imparting the essence of absence and demonstrating that silence can be more potent than love. It served as a lesson that guided me back to my authentic voice. I have discontinued my pursuit of resurrection and instead am crafting my resurrection into the narrative of my transformation.

May this chapter symbolize the past's burial and the present's emergence. A certain clarity emerges once one ceases hoping for reconciliation. It does not arrive with thunderous force; instead, it descends gently, akin to fog lifting from a field buried in mist for an extended period. One morning, one awakens, realizing they no longer await a text message to rectify the situation. They no longer monitor their tone to maintain harmony. They no longer beg their reflection to conform to their desires, to be more palatable, or to earn what should have been freely bestowed, finally.

This marks the commencement of healing. Healing is not ostentatious or dramatic. It is not a grand declaration or a cinematic confrontation. Sometimes, it involves choosing not to answer the phone or to attend one last gathering. It consists of embracing the quiet moments when no one else is observing. It is the whisper that assures one that they have endured enough, that they have held on long enough, and that they have shed sufficient.

Slowly and imperceptibly, one begins to breathe again. A new life emerges, not centered around the remnants of the past, but around the nascent possibilities within oneself. A life where one's worth is not measured by proximity to individuals who never truly recognized them. A life where one's presence is not merely tolerated but honored. A life where one's soul no longer seeks room at someone else's table, for they are finally constructing their own.

That dinner, once a source of pain, served as a funeral for the version of oneself who relentlessly shrank to accommodate the expectations of others. It was a farewell to the boy who believed loyalty entailed remaining in environments that drained his spirit. It was a bid adieu to the echo that mistakenly identified itself as a voice. Anger and waiting have dissipated. I am departing, not to seek retribution, but to liberate myself.

Sometimes, the most radical act is to cease returning to the scene of harm and instead cultivate gardens where graves once stood.

I did not merely survive that meal; I was reborn by it. Between the final bite and the final silence, a memory resurfaced, a memory of who I truly am. This time, I will ensure that memory remains etched in my consciousness.

Chapter 12
The Picture on the Mantle
"Sometimes you think time will change things-until you realize it hasn't changed a thing."

$\mathcal{N}$ot long ago, during last Christmas, I entered the house as always during the holiday season, harboring hope and apprehension for the customary heaviness that permeates the atmosphere. The familiar surroundings remained unchanged, the same walls, the same air, and the inescapable tension that simmers beneath the surface of forced normalcy.

Amidst the customary display of "important" items on the mantle above the fireplace, I noticed a framed photograph. It depicted Mickey Mouse holding a "Merry Christmas" sign. My brother had arranged for its creation while incarcerated, presumably as a gesture of familial remembrance. At first glance, the photograph appeared innocuous and even thoughtful. However, upon closer inspection, my heart ached as I read the names inscribed upon it: my brothers, my parents, and notably my name absent.

Standing there, transfixed by the photograph, I felt a profound sense of invisibility in the place that should have felt like home. No one noticed my absence, commented on the omission, or even paused to question the lack of my name. The photograph remained unremarked upon, as if it were an integral part of the family's identity.

In a way, this silence was even more painful than any overt rejection. It was a subtle yet profound erasure, a message conveyed without words or gestures. The photograph reminded me that, despite my growth, change, and evolution, I remained an outsider, a spectator in their lives.

Each time I passed that mantle that day, the message grew louder, echoing through my mind: even after everything, you still do not belong in their picture. It was not merely a cartoon drawing; it embodied the underlying sentiment, that time had not altered their perception of me.

They found ways to remind me of my exclusion, subtle reminders that lingered in the shadows of my existence. As I walked away from the situation, I remained silent, recognizing the futility of attempting to address it. Would they acknowledge my concerns? Would they dismiss them, laugh at my attempts to bring them to their attention, or feign indifference? The energy required to seek clarification was lacking. Therefore, I chose to keep my feelings to myself.

Later, as I bid farewell to that house, I made a silent yet resolute promise to myself: I would never again seek a place where I am not valued.

This occurred last Christmas, not years ago or in a distant past. It was a stark reminder that not all relationships warrant another chance simply because of shared blood ties. I am constructing my legacy, a mantle that will only display the names and faces of individuals who have chosen to value me. These people have made an effort to see and love me unconditionally; the essence of what family should embody. No one is excluded from this cherished display.

There are instances when one may believe they are invisible, only to be discovered by someone unexpectedly. It was not always a dramatic or public display of support. Sometimes, it was more subtle, more tender, and more human. One such instance occurred during middle school, when I grappled with burdens that no child should bear. My home was a chaotic environment, and my school was a noisy one. Without the vocabulary to express my needs at the time, I instinctively sought refuge when the weight became overwhelming. One day, I excused myself from class without a note or explanation, unsure of my destination. I sat in Mrs. Wallace's art room, sat, and remained silent. She did not inquire about my reasons or attempt to send me back. Instead, she allowed me to be there.

Later, I discovered that she had communicated with my teacher, informing them that I was experiencing difficulties and that she would monitor my progress. The term "monitor" has remained with me, not because it evoked an official or disciplinary connotation, but because, in her care, it acquired a sacred significance. She did not merely supervise me; she witnessed my journey. The hushed atmosphere in that room provided me with an unspoken solace, a profound sense of peace, presence, and the freedom to exist without the burden of performance or explanation. Although the specific content of the artwork on that day escapes my memory, I vividly recall the atmosphere. The stillness, the gentle scratching of pencils on paper, and the aroma of acrylic paint created a sanctuary within the classroom. Mrs. Wallace's movements around the room were guided by tranquility rather than the traditional classroom dynamics. In that quietude, I discovered a profound resource beyond mere encouragement. I found safety paramount for a child in a state of survival. Mrs. Wallace never delivered a speech emphasizing resilience or assuring me of my future success. However, her actions and silence spoke volumes. That moment marked one of the initial instances when I recognized the possibility of overcoming my challenges. Although the exact timing of my recovery remained uncertain, I held onto that glimmer of hope.

Years later, her memory continues visit me, not solely as a teacher but as a silent protector in a world that rarely offers solace. She did not owe me anything; she was neither a family member nor a therapist. She was simply a woman who recognized a child struggling to maintain his composure. Instead of demanding an explanation, she gave him a chair and a moment to compose himself. I wonder if she ever comprehended the profound impact of her actions. The storm details may fade for those raised in chaos, but the memory of finding shelter remains etched in our minds. We recall the tone of a voice that never imposed expectations, the comfort of someone who chose to sit with us as we unraveled quietly. That is precisely what Mrs. Wallace did. She did not offer me healing; she gave me time to gather my composure, feel safe, and be. That memory, encapsulated in her art room, the gentle clinking of paint jars, and the aroma of chalk and canvas, became a lifeline that I carried into adulthood. Even now, when I enter a room and being unwanted or hear the subtle sting of exclusion, I return to that sanctuary in my mind. I mentally recline in that hard plastic chair, close my eyes, and inhale the stillness she imparts. In a way, I draw strength from a moment that did not seek applause but saved me. It is remarkable how an individual's kindness can resonate for decades, while those who share our blood may pass us by unnoticed.

Mrs. Wallace was never included on our family Christmas list, nor was her name displayed above a mantle. However, her presence holds a greater significance in my narrative than others. I have realized that titles or traditions do not solely determine family; it is about the individuals who demonstrate their presence when our souls are at their wits' end.

As I create my version of home, where I hang my cherished photographs and fill the shelves with stories that resonate with me, her presence will be applied, not through a physical picture, but through the peace she instilled in me. She reminded me that I have been seen, even in my most vulnerable moments. In return for the room she made for me, I now strive to create a space for others. This legacy is the one I carry forward.

Chapter 13
Thanksgiving in the Hill Country

"Sometimes the people who were supposed to protect you are the same ones who turned away."

Thanksgiving was supposed to be about family, gathering, tradition, and gratitude. For me, Thanksgiving meant driving to the Hill Country-where the air was colder, heavier. A place I never felt safe. Every year, like clockwork, we packed up and drove for hours to visit my dad's side of the family. The road was long and winding, lined with trees and stretches of silence. I remember staring out the car window as a kid, feeling uneasy before we arrived. Something in my stomach always tightened when we pulled up to that house. I couldn't explain it then, but I know now that was my intuition. My soul knew what my mind couldn't name yet.

The house was always loud with relatives, food smells spilling from the kitchen, and laughter echoing through the walls. There was a dark corner in that house that no one saw. A shadow that followed me. My uncle. Every time we went there, it happened. He would wait until the adults were gone, busy, or distracted. He would block the door. His presence was a wall I couldn't get past. I was young, too young to fight or even understand. All I knew was the fear, the confusion, the shame, and the silence...always the silence. It happened year after year, and no one noticed. Not my mom. Not my dad. Not anyone in that crowded house full of family. Because no one was looking, and would they have done anything if they had been?

Years later, the truth finally surfaced. My parents eventually discovered what had been going on all those Thanksgivings in the Hill Country. There was no moment of righteous anger on my behalf. No one grabbed me and said, "I'm so sorry this happened to you." Instead, it was quiet. Uncomfortable. Brushed over. And somehow... I was the one who ended up feeling blamed.

I don't know exactly what was said to the other family members. I was too young to grasp it fully. All I knew was that the air around me felt heavier and more hostile after the truth came out. There were no apologies, protection, or justice, just a feeling that I had done something wrong.

That's the part that haunts me the most, not just what he did. But the after. The way the adults, those who were supposed to keep me safe handled it with the same silence they'd wrapped everything else in. The message was clear: We don't talk about it. We don't deal with it. We move on and pretend it didn't happen.

So, I did what I always did. I buried it. I buried the fear, the anger, the questions. I buried the feeling of being betrayed not just by the man who hurt me, but by the people who should've stood between me and the harm. But here's what I've learned: When you bury something that deep, it doesn't disappear. It grows roots. Roots that twist into shame. Into self-doubt. Into a lifelong question of worth. It shows up in the way you trust. In the way you flinch. In the way you walk into a room and scan for danger before you even realize you're doing it.

It's taken years even to say these words out loud. Years of realizing it wasn't my fault. Years to understand that his actions didn't define me or their silence.

As an adult, I look back at that boy in the Hill Country and see him differently. I saw a child who was brave enough to keep breathing. I know a soul that refused to be broken, even when the world gave him every reason to shatter. I see someone who survived not because anyone saved him, but because something deep inside knew his story wasn't over yet. If you've ever been through something like that, I want you to hear me: It was not your fault. You didn't deserve it, and the silence of others does not mean your pain wasn't real.

Those Thanksgivings in the Hill Country are part of my story. They are not the whole story, because the same boy who endured all that? He's the man writing this now, and he's not silent anymore.

For a long time, I thought healing meant forgetting. I could outrun the memories if I moved forward fast enough, far enough. If I built a life that looked good from the outside, I wouldn't have to feel the rot underneath it. You don't outrun what lives in your nervous system. You don't outgrow what was never given space to be grieved. For a while, I didn't even realize how much of me was still stuck in that house. In that room. In that moment. Not just the boy who was hurt, but the boy who wasn't helped. That's the part no one talks about. People focus on the event, the "what happened.". The real wound sometimes isn't just abuse. It's the abandonment that followed. The quiet betrayal from those who were supposed to fight for you and didn't. The realization that the people you needed most were either too scared, ashamed, or selfish to say: You didn't deserve that, and I failed you. So, I became my protector. My witness. My courtroom and judge. I replayed the past like a case file, wondering if I was overreacting, if maybe it wasn't that bad, if perhaps I was the problem. That's what trauma does. It doesn't just steal your innocence. It steals your clarity. But now? I see things. That little boy was never overreacting. He was overpowered and he didn't need to prove anything to deserve safety. He didn't need to explain his pain to be believed, and neither do you.

If you're reading this and have been through something like it, where the room was packed, nobody saw you, where the voices were loud, but no one spoke up for you, I want you to know something no one told me: Your pain deserves a name. Your memory deserves a witness, and your younger self deserves justice, even if it comes decades later, even if it comes in the form of your voice saying, that was not okay. Healing didn't come to me in a moment. It came in waves within messy conversations, therapy sessions where I said things out loud for the first time and then sat in the silence afterward, stunned that the world didn't collapse. It came in deep breaths and hard truths. It came in replacing blame with compassion for myself. I didn't fail anyone, they failed me, and I am no longer carrying that shame for them. So no, I don't go to the Hill Country anymore. I don't pretend or perform. I don't smile to keep the peace. I create peace wherever I go because I earned it and the man I am today? He doesn't need anyone's permission to protect the boy he used to be. He's already doing it.

These days, Thanksgiving looks different. I don't drive down winding roads to houses that hold ghosts. I don't sit in rooms where my silence is mistaken for peace. I don't pass the mashed potatoes with a smile while swallowing the weight of

90

everything left unsaid. Now, I am creating my table. Sometimes it's small. Sometimes it's just a few people who've earned the right to sit beside me. Sometimes it's me and a quiet moment of gratitude for how far I've come, but it's mine and there's power in that. Healing isn't always loud or public, sometimes, it's subtle. It's saying no to traditions that broke you. It's choosing solitude over performance. It's realizing that you don't owe anyone a seat in your life just because they share your blood.

I used to think I needed closure to move on. That someone had to say the right words or finally admit the wrong. I've learned that sometimes the only closure you get is the life you choose to build after the damage. So, I've stopped waiting. I no longer measure my healing by what they understand or acknowledge. I measure it by how I show up for myself, by how I refuse to shrink, love without conditions, starting with me. Each year, around this time, I do something small to honor the boy I was. I light a candle. I cook something that makes me feel good. I play music that fills the silence with beauty, and I whisper a quiet promise to him: You made it. You're safe now. You'll never be forgotten again.

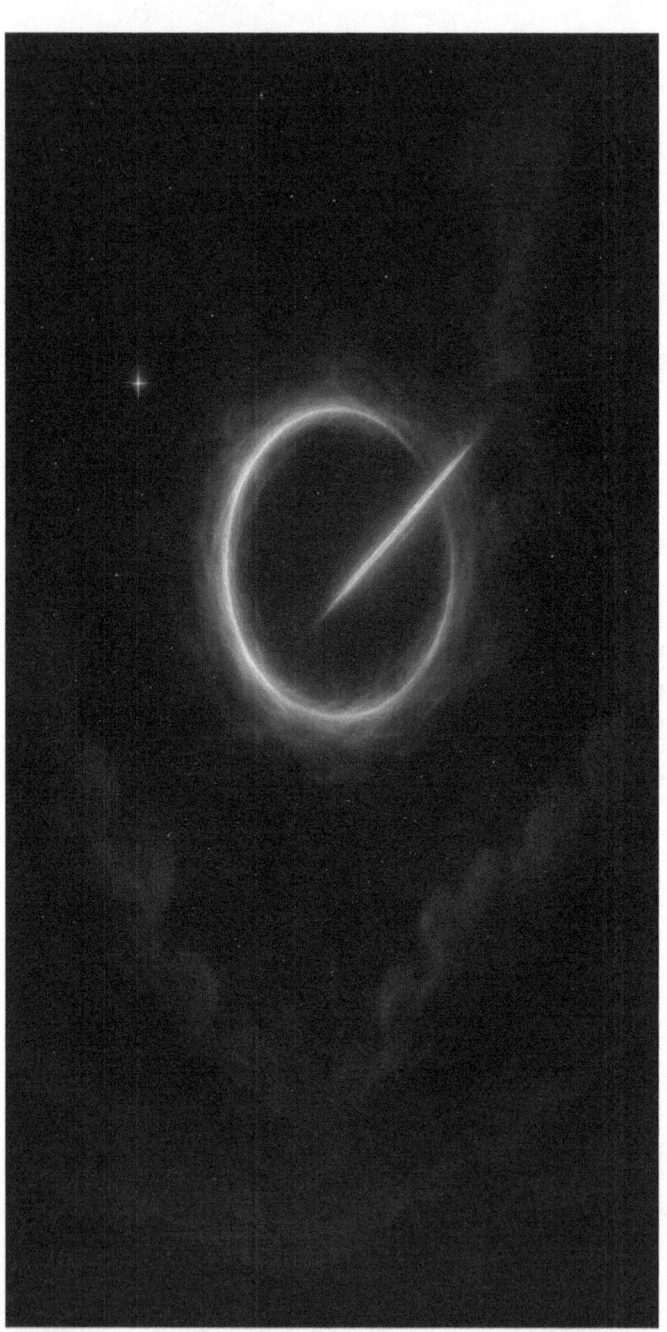

Chapter 14
When the Universe Spoke Back

*"Sometimes the universe doesn't speak in
thunder. It speaks in echoes—through people,
timing, and signs—reminding you that your
voice is part of something divine."*

$\mathcal{T}$here comes a point in your journey when
you're not just writing your story anymore, you're
being written into something larger. I didn't expect
the writing process to hit so hard. I thought I'd be
pouring out memories and moving on. Instead, it felt
like cutting open a vein, letting every unspoken word,
every hidden ache, every unresolved thread spill onto
the page. I kept asking myself: Did I go too far? Did
I share too much? Did I do the right thing?

There were moments I wanted to stop.
Moments when the guilt crept in, whispering,
"You're betraying your family. You're making them
look bad. Maybe you're the problem after all." That's
the part no one tells you about healing, it doesn't just
come with clarity. It comes with a storm and then,
right when I was second-guessing everything, the
universe spoke.

Out of nowhere, my friend Zach called me.
There was no reason, no agenda. His voice on the
other end says, "I just want to tell you how proud I
am of you... This book? It's powerful. It's inspiring.
You've become so strong." My jaw dropped. He
couldn't have known the mental space I was in, but

he said exactly what I needed to hear, down to the syllables. It was like the Divine reached through him to anchor me back in place. Not even an hour later, Natalie my friend from the military messaged me. She told me how much she admired the courage it took to tell this story. She said it reminded her of her strength and gave her hope. That's not a coincidence. That's confirmation and this wasn't the first time.

I've had moments on this path where something far beyond me made its presence known, like the time on the cruise when I gave a message to a woman I'd never met. All I knew was that the scent of Brut washed over me so strong I thought it was part of the ship's air system. When I spoke up and described it, she froze. Her eyes welled up with tears. "That was my dad's scent," she whispered, trembling. "You just described him exactly. She wept, and in that moment, I knew I wasn't just a man on vacation. I was a vessel and something sacred was speaking through me. It happens too often to ignore. The signs, the synchronized numbers, the people who call right when I'm about to give up. The dreams that turn into moments. The words appear in songs, books, and strangers' mouths, like they've been planted there, waiting for me to arrive, and then there are the TikTok comments. I remember one that stopped me cold. A stranger wrote: "I don't know why, but your words healed something in me I didn't know was broken." How do you explain that? How do you explain being seen by people you've never met, being felt by those who've never touched you? You don't. You listen and you keep going because the universe has its ways. It doesn't always shout. Sometimes it whispers through friends. Sometimes it cries through strangers. Sometimes it clutches your heart mid-sentence, as if to say: "Keep writing. You're not just telling your truth. You're unlocking someone else's."

This chapter, this whole journey was never just mine. It was always ours and this moment right here? It's not the end. It's the echo of something that began long before me and will continue long after.

When I think about the truth—that this story was never just mine. I realize how deeply intertwined we all are. My words are stitched together with threads I didn't even know existed until they pulled taut.

Sometimes it's a conversation in passing, sometimes it's how a stranger's eyes linger a little longer than usual, as if they recognize something familiar in me. Sometimes, it's in the quiet moments, when I'm alone at my desk, and a thought drops into my spirit so suddenly, so precisely, that I know it didn't come from me. That's the thing about the echo, it doesn't belong to the one who speaks first. It belongs to every ear it reaches, every heart it strikes, every life it changes in ways I'll never fully see.

I've had people reach out and tell me my words made them feel less alone, not because I solved their pain, but because I named it, I gave it shape, and sometimes, seeing the outline of something is enough to remind you it can be faced. Writing has taught me this: you never truly know where your story will end. You know that you'll never find out if you silence it, so I keep going. It's not because it's easy, not because I have all the answers, but somewhere, someone is sitting in the same darkness I once knew and maybe, just maybe, my light can reach them. This is the responsibility of the echo, and I've decided to carry it. There's a pull inside me now knowing that once you've touched something greater than yourself, you can't go back to pretending it's not there.

I've seen what happens when you tell the truth, even when your voice shakes. I've felt the shift in a room when a story lands in the exact heart it was meant for. I've witnessed people breathe differently not because their circumstances changed in that moment, but because something inside them did. I want that for this book, not headlines or hollow praise. Impact Real, soul-level impact. I'm not naïve enough to think my words will save everyone. Maybe they'll save someone, and perhaps that's enough.

When I started writing, I thought I was trying to make sense of my past. Now I see I was also writing a lifeline for the ones who would come after me, for the ones who would see themselves in these pages and feel a quiet strength whisper back: "If they survived it, maybe I can too." I don't know where this journey will take me from here. I know that whatever comes next, I'll step into it with the same open hands that wrote these pages because the echo isn't done yet and neither am I. When you've been through fire, people think the story ends when you walk out of the flames. The truth is that the real story begins in the quiet after. That's where the rebuilding happens, where the meaning settles in. That's where you finally understand that everything you carried, every scar and shadow, wasn't just for you, it was for someone else's light to find its way through.

I don't believe in accidents, chanced encounters, random timing, or meaningless words anymore. I believe in alignment. I believe in the divine threading of lives together in ways we may never fully understand on this side of heaven. This book is my offering to that thread. My way of saying: I was here. I lived this and I left a map for anyone still lost in the dark, and if even one person finds their way because of it, then every page, every tear, every sleepless night spent wrestling with the truth… will have been worth it because the echo doesn't fade when the story ends.

It moves forward through the next heart, the next, and the next until the message that started in one voice becomes a chorus, and maybe that's the point. Maybe the story was never meant to stay mine at all.

Chapter 15
No Chimney, No Welcome
*"Even in a house full of people, I felt like the
unwanted one shoved under the stairs."*

$\mathcal{A}$s a child, I pondered the logistics of Santa
Claus's entry in the absence of a chimney. I recall
inquiring with my mother, who provided an
explanation that lacked coherence. Despite this, I
allowed the matter to pass. Children are adept at
maintaining belief in the supernatural, even when it
defies rational explanation. However, a lingering
sense persisted that I might not receive Santa's visit
after all. Even within the confines of my home and
under the same roof, I felt a profound sense of
alienation, lacking the belonging that seemed to elude
others.

As a child, I would watch Christmas movies,
narratives filled with warmth, family, and the promise
of second chances. However, the Harry Potter series
resonated with me the most, not due to its magical
elements or the Hogwarts school, but rather to its
portrayal of Harry's life under the stairs in the
Dursleys' house. This resonated deeply with my own
experiences. I felt like the child who was
metaphorically shoved into a closet while everyone
else in the household received genuine love. My
brothers were treated differently, not because they
were imperfect, but because they did not carry the
same burden as I did. They were not labeled as

mistakes, blamed for their existence, or subjected to the same level of silence. They were still considered part of the family even when they made errors. In contrast, I was relegated to the shadows.

Even the most subtle details revealed my exclusion: the gradual decline in the number of presents bearing my name. In contrast, the number of presents for my brothers remained constant, the lack of recognition for my achievements, and the pervasive silence that accompanied me, rather than smiles. As I matured, my anticipation for Christmas diminished. The allure of gifts, which I did not require, was overshadowed by their symbolic significance: inclusion, thoughtfulness, and acknowledgment of my presence. However, my reality was far different. Instead of receiving thoughtful gifts, I was often presented with mundane items such as candles or pillows, while others eagerly opened boxes filled with time and care.

This recollection evoked a profound sense of isolation within my family, the same to Harry's experience in the cupboard, observing others from afar while yearning to access their privileged experiences. The crux of the matter lay not only in the treatment I endured but also in the realization that no one else perceived the disparity in my treatment or the emotional distance I felt. The silence surrounding my situation was a form of violence, as it prevented me from expressing my feelings and seeking validation. Years passed, and I harbored a persistent hope for a moment that never materialized, a moment when they would acknowledge their shortcomings, express regret for their treatment, and recognize my worth. However, that elusive moment eluded me, culminating in the poignant absence of my name from the Christmas mantle last year.

Time, it seems, does not alter individuals who are resolute in their self-perception. Consequently, my perspective on Harry Potter has undergone a transformative shift. Unlike Harry, who remained confined to the shadows of his family's neglect for many years of his childhood, I discovered my destiny, a path that transcended my limitations. I have learned to forge my sense of magic, creating a sanctuary of belonging that is not contingent upon external validation or acceptance.

One moment in the Harry Potter series resonates deeply with me, notwithstanding the grand battles, spells, or the exhilarating experience of flying on a broomstick. In the quieter scenes, Harry finds solace sitting alone at Hogwarts, observing his fellow students engrossed in laughter, writing letters, and receiving gifts. From his perch on the sidelines, a sense of longing permeates his eyes yearning to belong, yet a lingering doubt that he does. This resonated profoundly with me, as I have personally experienced similar feelings. Surrounded by people still feeling like outsiders, navigating familiar spaces that never felt like home. Expressing the ache behind a smile, yearning for someone to perceive the depth of one's emotions, and grappling with the possibility that certain aspects of oneself may not be perceived as lovable. Harry's character transcended the mere label of "other," a child who was labeled before fully comprehending the reasons behind it. He was the one who bore the brunt of blame, mistreatment, and silence, and who was told to be grateful for the opportunity to be taken in.

In that line, I have heard its echoes throughout my life. It was not always spoken aloud; sometimes, it manifested in looks, sighs, and how I was treated instead of being addressed. The underlying message was unmistakable: you are fortunate to be alive. Like

Harry, I did not receive warm embraces or words of affirmation; instead, I faced conditions, comparisons, and subtle yet brutal reminders of my inferiority. However, Harry possessed an unbreakable spirit. Even when confined to that cupboard, subjected to derogatory labels, and deceived about his true identity, his essence remained unshaken. This resilience resonated within me as well. Even during Christmases when I felt invisible, when the gifts ceased, and when my name was omitted from a family photograph, a part of me, quiet, determined, and divine, refused to succumb to despair.

As Harry discovered his magical heritage, I uncovered my sacred connection: resilience, purpose, and a calling. Although I did not receive a letter from Hogwarts delivered by an owl, I gained something far more valuable: clarity. It revealed that I was never the problem; they could not love me in the way I deserved. This clarity empowered me to cease seeking their validation and instead focus on building my own life.

Previously, I sought their approval; now, I prioritize my peace. I no longer conform to their expectations but create my own narrative. Similarly to Harry, I have chosen my own family—not those who share my blood, but those who resonate with my heart. This is true magic: when you cease waiting to be chosen and embrace the power of self-selection.

In essence, Harry Potter's narrative transcended magic; it explored the concept of found family. Despite his humble beginnings under the stairs, he transcended that environment and found solace and belonging in those who recognized and embraced him. The choice to stand beside him was not compelled; it was driven by love and a desire to support him. This transformative act changed everything.

Love found me in a world where I had been overlooked, undervalued, and made to feel like a mistake for years. Real love, unconditional and unwavering, walked in and said, "You don't have to earn this; just be."

Tiffany and Mike have transcended friendship; they have become my sanctuary, my grounding. They welcomed me into their home as if it had always been mine, and their parents, from the very beginning, embraced me with open arms, as if they had been eagerly anticipating my arrival. There were no questions, no hesitations, only warmth and love.

Zach, he is the brother I never knew I could have. He never made me feel like a burden, and his presence alone instills a sense of safety. Our bond is unparalleled, built on mutual respect, loyalty, and a deep emotional connection.

and Eva—Oh, Eva. From high school to now, she has been my constant beacon of light. She is the mother figure I never had, yet I somehow felt her presence. She believed in me before I believed in myself, embodying wisdom, love, and a fiery spirit in every breath. She didn't just show me what a mother could be; she redefined it.

Then there's Lora and Bret. At a time when I felt adrift, uncertain of where to turn or where to find safety, they opened their doors and hearts. Their children call me Uncle, not out of obligation, but out of genuine love. When those little arms wrap around me and call my name with joy, something deep within me heals, and something buried is finally revealed. They are not alone on this journey; countless others have stepped in, becoming friends who became family, mentors who offered wisdom, and strangers who became anchors in moments of chaos.

Each of these individuals contributed a brick to the home I was constructing for my heart, not a physical structure, but a profound sense of belonging. A deep-rooted understanding that I am cherished, selected, and accepted. This family revealed what had always eluded me, and what makes their love truly remarkable is its unconditional nature. I did not need to prove my worth or justify my past. I had to be present, and they responded with grace. They embody the magic I sought, not the kind conjured by wands or spells, but the kind manifested through open doors, gentle arrivals, and the quiet, transformative act of being chosen.

Therefore, I no longer require a chimney or a place in someone else's narrative where I am merely tolerated. I have built my house with individuals who recognize and appreciate me.

They serve as constant reminders that I was never the unwanted one. I was the unclaimed miracle, the misjudged gift, the survivor with a vast purpose that intimidated those who could not embrace it. Now, I no longer await love to descend from a chimney. Instead, I widen the door and welcome it with open arms.

Chapter 16
The Marriage Was Real-So Was the Pain

"Sometimes the silence isn't about who you're with-it's about who you are. And sometimes, it's about more than one kind of betrayal."

When I got married, I thought maybe this would be the turning point for me and them. Maybe they might see that my love was real. It wasn't a phase or rebellion, or whatever they convinced themselves it was. Just maybe they might soften their hearts and show up, but they didn't.

At first, it was just a shift I couldn't name. The calls came less frequently, the conversations grew shorter, and the energy felt cold. Then, one day, it wasn't subtle anymore. It was silent. Weeks turned into months of silence.

For all his flaws, my ex-husband did try to connect with them. He was polite, asked questions, and wanted to bridge the gap. My mother was cold, ugly in the way only someone who refuses to see you as human can be. Finally, after months of nothing, she picked up the phone. Her reason?

"I don't like listening to him."

Flat. Emotionless. Not that he disrespected her or he did anything wrong. Just... "I don't like listening to him." I knew the truth. It wasn't about him; it was about me. No matter who I loved or how kind or careful or patient they were, it wouldn't have mattered. They didn't want to accept me.

Still, even knowing that, I held on to the marriage because, as broken as my family was, at least I believed this love was mine. At least he was supposed to be my safe place. Love is complicated, and people aren't always what you think they are. While dealing with my family's silence, I didn't realize another silence was creeping in, the kind you don't notice at first. The kind that feels like distance, but you can't name why. The lies. The betrayal. The truth I would later discover was that while I was fighting to hold onto us, he was already slipping away into something else.

I didn't know then that he had another life hidden behind his phone. I didn't realize that while I was trying to build a home with him, he was seeking validation elsewhere, through Grindr, messages, and things that shattered the foundation of what we had. I didn't know yet that the man I defended in front of my family would eventually hurt me in ways they never could.

At the time, I was juggling the pain from both sides. Trying to deal with parents who wouldn't accept me. Trying to hold on to a marriage that was already cracking in ways I didn't fully see. I thought the silence from my family was the only storm I was facing, but I was wrong. There was another storm brewing right beside me and I was about to find out just how deep betrayal can cut-even when it comes from the person who swore they loved you.

What they didn't see was what it cost me to stay. They'll never understand how many nights I lay in that bed, next to a man who felt miles away, trying to convince myself that love was going through a rough patch. Maybe if I gave more, loved harder, he'd return to me fully, not just in body, but in truth.

What do you do when your safe place becomes a stage? When you realize the person, you married learned how to smile through lies? How can you say the right things publicly while doing everything wrong behind closed doors? He wasn't just absent, he was performing, smiling in group photos, and holding my hand in public. Then, he turned around and used that same hand to open his phone and chase something else. It wasn't just cheating. It was the gaslighting, the denial.

The way he'd flip the script and make me feel crazy for noticing things I wasn't supposed to see. He'd call me paranoid, accuse me of being dramatic. Say I was "too sensitive.". While his phone buzzed from names, I'd never hear him speak aloud. What hurts more than the betrayal is how easy it was for him to destroy me with his words afterward. He didn't just leave me. He dragged my name behind him. Made jokes. Spread rumors. Painted me out to be the unstable one. The emotional one. The problem. And the worst part? People believed him. People I once called friends. People who stood at our wedding. People who had seen me bend over backwards to protect a man who didn't even flinch when it was time to hurt me. I watched my reputation crumble while he played the victim, and no one stopped him. No one pulled me aside to say, "That doesn't sound like you." No one stepped up and called it what it was: abuse dressed in charm. Eventually, some admitted they saw that he had been distant. He said he had checked out the marriage long before it ended. That they "knew something wasn't right." But where were those words when I needed them? Where was the support when I was fighting to make sense of the gaslighting, the lies, the emotional warfare? Where was the truth when I was drowning in his fiction? They stayed quiet and their silence wasn't neutral.

It was a second betrayal. Because when someone sits back and watches your character be dismantled and doesn't say a word,

they become complicit. I didn't just lose a husband. I lost my reputation. My community. My sense of safety in people I thought would always have my back. The irony was he walked away clean, untouched, still liked, still supported; while I was left to rebuild myself from the wreckage of a story I didn't write. But here's what I know now: I may have been lied to. I may have been left. I may have been dragged through the mud, but I never lost my truth. One day, when the lights fade, the charm wears off, and the lies dry up—he'll realize something he couldn't see through his ego: He didn't leave behind a mistake. He lost someone who would've stood before a fire for him and that's not something you recover from.

It's been three years. Three years since the silence. Since the betrayal, since I stood in the wreckage of what I thought was forever, and realized I was the only one trying to build it and still, here I am.

Not broken.
Not bitter.
Not perfect.
But healing.

I'm healing in places I didn't know could heal. Soft in ways I never thought I'd be again. The hardest part wasn't leaving the marriage. It was unlearning the belief that I wasn't worthy of better. For a long time, I thought what I had was the best I could get. That maybe the scraps were love. That perhaps love always came with pain: with performance, pretending.

I know better now what real love feels like. I've become it myself. I know how to speak gently to my own heart. I know how to set boundaries without guilt. I know what peace sounds like in my own home, and I know what I'll never settle for again.

Am I still single? Yes. But I'm not searching the way I used to. I'm not chasing. I'm not proving. I'm not bending myself into versions that someone else can accept. Because now, I understand: The right one will never need me to shrink. He'll recognize the strength in my scars. He'll see my tenderness not as a weakness, but as proof that I've survived without going numb. He won't just want to be loved, he'll know how to love back. When that day comes to say, "I do", it won't be to fill a void. It'll be to build something sacred, rooted and real. Until then, I'm not waiting, I'm living. I'm letting things unravel and unfold in their divine timing. Because now I trust that what's meant for me doesn't need to be chased. My love story isn't behind me, it's still being written and when it finally arrives, it won't have to compete with ghosts or heal wounds it didn't cause. It'll feel like breath that exhale in and out and this time I'll know I'm safe there.

Chapter 17

A Silence with a Name: Shame

"Some endings don't come with closure. They come with shattered glass and silence that speaks louder than words."

On the night that marked the culmination of our relationship, we found ourselves in the living room, the weight of weeks and months of suspicion and distance palpable. I had confronted him once more, inquiring about his fidelity. Despite his adamant denial, his unwavering gaze and resolute "No" were enough to shatter the remaining illusions I had clung to. My intuition, however, remained steadfast in its conviction. I had reached my breaking point and declared my desire for a divorce. Barefoot, I vividly recall the sensation of the cool floor beneath my feet, providing a grounding anchor amidst the chaos of that moment. In that instant, he approached the wall where our marriage certificate was framed and hanging. Without uttering a word, he tore it down, shattering it into fragments scattered across the floor like shrapnel. Before I could react, the glass fragments pierced the soles of my feet, drawing blood.

Remarkably, I remained silent, unable to yell, cry, or even speak. Instead, I fixed my gaze upon the broken frame on the floor, at the certificate that once symbolized love, commitment, and partnership, now reduced to ruins, devoid of any semblance of meaning. In that moment, I comprehended the finality of our relationship. That night, I departed barefoot and bleeding, venturing into the darkness without a second glance. I refrained from answering his calls, denying him the opportunity to engage in another conversation. I had made my decision, and I was determined to move forward. However, it is essential to acknowledge that endings are not always straightforward.

Amidst the process of grieving the dissolution of our marriage and attempting to rebuild my shattered sense of self, I discovered the truth. He had taken decisive action, blocking me on Facebook and every other platform, as if I had never existed. To my astonishment, I found that the individual I had suspected and believed to be the cause of his infidelity was now officially connected with him on Facebook, less than two months after that night.

The most poignant revelation was that we were still legally married at this discovery. The legal proceedings for divorce had not yet commenced. Despite being legally bound as name partners, I discovered that my partner had already moved in his new partner, the same man with whom he had been unfaithful and abandoned me. While I anticipated this would culminate our relationship, it was a mere prelude to further complications.

Contrary to my expectations, anger was not the most overwhelming emotion. Instead, a profound sense of silence and heavy, hollow shame enveloped me. This shame was not the conventional kind that acknowledges wrongdoing, but rather a profound acknowledgment of giving my heart to someone who had never reciprocated its value. The echo of betrayal lingered, causing me to question my worth, doubt my instincts, and grieve for the person involved and the version of myself who had believed in their fidelity.

I have come to realize that the infidelity and subsequent lies were solely his responsibility. The broken glass, the public humiliation, and the physical pain were all his actions. None of these events resonated deeply within my soul, as I had approached the relationship with full commitment and unconditional love. Even though he had disregarded this love, its authenticity remained unwavering.

This experience has made me stronger and more discerning. It has taught me the boundaries I will never tolerate again and emphasized that love is only truly love when it is reciprocal. Moreover, it reminded me that sometimes, the most effective form of closure is to move forward without dwelling on the past. Despite gaining this profound insight, I still found myself revisiting old photographs, wondering about the version of myself who had believed in such a flawed relationship.

The individual who smiled beside him maintained their unwavering belief and held onto the notion that love entailed sacrifice, even when I was the sole one making sacrifices. Healing did not occur in a single, transformative revelation; instead, it unfolded gradually, through incremental moments and silent decisions to persevere, even when the weight of despair seemed insurmountable. There were nights when I sat in silence, rather than fleeing from it, and instead, I allowed it to speak. It revealed truths that I had long suppressed: that I had rationalized disrespect, mistook chaos for passion, and conflated longevity with love. Despite the arduousness of accepting these truths, I had remained in the relationship for an extended period, not due to weakness, but out of loyalty. I had believed that love was a struggle, a battle to maintain. However, one should not have to fight to keep someone.

There exists a distinction between fighting for love and fighting because love has vanished, and you are hesitant to acknowledge its absence. Eventually, the silence transformed from a haunting presence into a catalyst for healing. It no longer reminded me of what I had lost; instead, it reminded me of what I had reclaimed. My voice, my peace, my power.

With each step forward, I began to transcend my former self, becoming someone I had not been in a considerable amount of time. Someone who did not require permission to radiate light, did not apologize for their heart, and no longer tie their worth to the inability of others to perceive it.

Therefore, if you have ever experienced the pain of walking barefoot through shattered glass, discarded and witnessed someone else being celebrated in your place, if you have been left with only silence and shame, please listen to me when I say this:

"Their actions do not define you."

You are the architect of your future, and if you have chosen to embark on the journey of healing and rebuilding, then know that you possess the power to shape your destiny. To love again, you have already achieved victory, even if the pain persists, the memories linger, and silence remains your companion. This silence reminds you of your resilience and strength, becoming your anthem. Nothing is more potent than surviving an attempt to silence you and choosing to speak anyway. Healing is not a sudden process; it unfolds in fragments. These fragments may manifest in quiet mornings when the ache is less pronounced, during long drives with music that drowns out the memories, or in new friendships that do not demand your shrinking or apology for your profound emotions. Healing also involves rebuilding a self, not just a physical home, but a sense of self.

I recall the moment I laughed without thinking of him. It was the first time I looked in the mirror, I did not see the discarded remnants of our relationship; instead, I saw the survivor within me. That version of me? He never encountered him, never experienced the privilege of such a connection. That was the actual loss, he lost someone who would have stood by him during challenging times, someone who possessed unwavering loyalty. He lost the kind of love that people fervently seek, and he squandered it as if it were disposable. I did not lose; I shed, outgrew, and was never ruined; I was refined.

That silence that once kept me awake at night? I gave it a name, reclaiming my voice from its grasp. I transformed it into this chapter, hoping that anyone reading, anyone silently suffering as I once did, would find solace in these words:

"You are not the broken glass."

"You are not the betrayer."

"You are not what they left behind."

"You are what emerges from the wreckage, and that is something sacred."

Chapter 18
Messages from the Other Side

"Those we love never truly leave us. They walk beside us in whispers and in signs, just beyond the veil"

$\mathcal{F}$ollowing my divorce, I experienced a profound sense of grief beyond the loss of my ex-husband. I grieved betrayal, parental silence, and the profound shattering of my life. It felt as though I had been stripped bare of my former self. At my lowest point, a glimmer of hope emerged. It commenced with unexplainable emotions, chills, and familiar whispers. Occasionally, dreams felt eerily real, and memories would suddenly resurface. Initially, I dismissed these sensations, but they persisted.

In February 2025, during a cruise, I encountered a stranger. We engaged in a casual conversation. I noticed a distinct masculine scent -Brut aftershave. It struck me with a profound impact. A clear message resonated within me. Despite my initial hesitation, I inquired, "Is someone attempting to convey a message to you?" She froze, her eyes filled with tears, and then she wept. She revealed that the scent belonged to her father.

The message resonated deeply within me, leaving no room for coincidence. I understood that a man she loved had passed away, yet his spirit remained. I transcended the boundaries between worlds, becoming a beacon of friendship for that stranger. Such encounters serve as reminders that souls connect and confirm my profound feelings. The veil between realms is not as impenetrable as we may believe. Love transcends death; sometimes, the departed choose unexpected vessels to convey their messages.

I have received numerous messages, emotions, and a profound understanding. At first, I was overwhelmed by the question, "Why me?" However, I realized that my emotional vulnerability made me receptive to holding and comprehending someone else's pain.

I perceive these gifts as divine blessings, love endures, connections find a way, and I was never truly alone during my darkest hour. Individuals often inquire about the source of my knowledge, and sometimes, I cannot provide a definitive explanation. Nevertheless, I am sure of the authenticity of these experiences because they have healed others and me. This awakening transformed my pain into a purposeful force. I ceased questioning, "Why me?" and instead focused on, "What can I do?" Following this inner guidance led me to where I was meant to be.

Previously, I believed that these gifts belonged to individuals who possessed exceptional abilities or were groomed to navigate between worlds, not to someone who had endured the profound scars of grief. Perhaps that is why this extraordinary experience occurred. Broken hearts possess unmistakable signals. Love and loss create a frequency that resonates with the spirit, guiding it towards healing and connection. Messages did not always accompany perfume. Occasionally, a memory or name lingered in my mind. I once held a woman's hand and felt her brother's playful energy. The message was straightforward: "Convey to her that I endured no suffering." She gasped, her knees buckled, and healing commenced. This was not about performance but about presence, trust, and creating space for someone who needed to know they were never forgotten.

One evening, alone, I inquired, "Am I destined to fulfill this purpose?" Warmth and tranquility enveloped me, accompanied by a whisper in my spirit: "This is the reason for your survival." I ceased resisting this purpose.

I do not assert myself as a psychic or prophet. I do not possess all the answers but am attuned to my feelings and perceptions. I have witnessed tears and softened hearts as they realized their loved ones had transitioned. Sacred messages arrive when no one seeks them, grief is not audible, and healing manifests through silence. Spirit operates differently: not always with thunderous displays, but with a whisper that only a wounded heart can perceive. In those moments, I recognize that we are never truly alone; we are constantly communicated with and must listen. I no longer subscribe to the concept of coincidences.

For many years, I dismissed occurrences such as mere timing, projection, or grief. However, patterns became undeniable, a language beneath language, a frequency beneath noise, speaking when our world becomes quiet. My world had grown hushed.

Following my divorce, the dissolution of my identity, and the erosion of my belief in family, I felt adrift, bereft, and utterly devoid of purpose. It was then, something transcendent whispered: a song at the opportune moment, a feather landing during a conversation about surrender, a crow calling outside my window on a day of tears, a dream borrowed from another realm. These were not mere memories or delusions; they were messages. The more I honored them, the more they facilitated healing. I ceased seeking proof and demanding evidence. Instead, I began to listen.

Grief opens us to the realm of the spirit. I would empathize with another's sorrow, hear songs intended for others, and receive profound insights. Occasionally, I would utter these insights aloud, and they always resonated. I would gaze into the eyes of strangers and witness their emotional turmoil, not to impress, but to rekindle a connection they believed had been lost. The intangible became tangible, and I became the conduit for this connection. Initially, I dismissed these experiences as mere figments of my imagination, but the more I resisted them, the more they persisted.

I would discern whose pain remained unspoken, hear names whispered in my mind, until they became the precise names someone needed. I would dream of individuals I had not thought of in years, only to discover that they had passed away. This was not a product of my imagination; it was an invitation.

By embracing this gift, I realized that it was not about becoming a psychic or medium. It was about being receptive, carrying messages, remaining steadfast when someone else's world crumbled, and allowing my pain to serve as a gateway, not a dead end. I ceased to flee from the unseen and welcomed it with open arms, for it was an old friend.

These moments, these messages, belong to all of us. They only speak in silence when another significant loss occurs. I have been advised to remain private, as I am apprehensive of judgment and labeling. However, I have squandered time worrying about individuals who never comprehended my authenticity. My purpose is not to conform to societal expectations but to be authentic. If that entails acknowledging my encounters with the departed, receiving messages in the darkness, or finding solace from a long-lost loved one, then so be it. Let them harbor doubts, laughter, or disregard for me. They were absent when I heard my grandmother's voice, felt a stranger's comfort, or recognized that my struggles were transformative.

I have experienced significant losses; my marriage, the silence of my parents, and the pain and suffering, because these messages found their way into an empty life, not in a life filled with fulfillment, but in a void. Only an empty vessel can be filled.

When I experience that distinctive sensational tug in my chest, an inexplicable name, or a phrase that unexpectedly comes to mind, I no longer question it. I take a deep breath, pause, and speak because somewhere, someone is listening. Perhaps they require a message from the beyond, and I was destined to deliver it.

I did not seek this gift of perceiving thoughts and emotions others cannot comprehend, sensing energy within a room, or navigating the world attuned to a frequency most people overlook. However, perhaps the most valuable gifts are those we would never choose, they transform our essence, not merely our actions.

This gift has transformed me, not into an entirely new person, but into a trustworthy individual. I no longer enter a room seeking proof; instead, I approach with awareness, a gentle spirit, and an open chest, prepared to receive whatever comes my way. Whether it is a whisper, a knowing, or a moment of profound stillness that feels as though someone has paused the world, there are times when nothing transpires. Nevertheless, the stillness itself becomes the message. Not every revelation necessitates loudness; not every sign is a thunderbolt. Some are mere feathers in the wind, landing precisely where they are meant to.

Being a vessel is not about performance; it is about presence and availability, not only to the unseen, but also to the individual's right in front of me, who carry wounds they cannot articulate. These individuals may laugh excessively to conceal their loss. They may require someone to perceive them for who they truly are. There is no guidebook for this journey. There is no certification, checklist, or blueprint. All that matters is trust, surrender, and the gradual unfolding of your spirit.

You realize that the version of yourself who once sought salvation has become a sanctuary for others. If you had been told years ago that you would stand before strangers and utter the words of the departed, you would have laughed. Even you being told that you would find solace in holding others' grief, you would have responded with a sense of inadequacy. However, we find our strength in the places where we once felt shattered. When we allow the light in, cease to conceal ourselves, and cease to explain, we discover that we are the message.

If you have ever experienced an unexplainable sensation, such as a dream of a deceased loved one accompanied by tears upon waking, or a gentle breeze caressing your skin as if it recognized your name, it is essential to acknowledge and embrace these experiences. Could you not dismiss or ignore them? These enduring bonds of love transcend time and space, the unbroken threads that connect us to the beyond. The other side is not merely reaching out to greet us; it offers solace and reassurance, reminding us that we are never truly alone. This truth has been constant throughout our lives and will continue to be so in the future.

Chapter 19

When the Bottle Spoke Louder Than Me

"The bottle never healed me; it only muted my truth until it screamed in other ways"

When you drown pain, it waits. After my divorce, I thought the worst was over. Walking barefoot, bleeding, and never looking back seemed challenging.

Leaving isn't just about freedom; it's emptiness, which can be loud. I didn't want to feel betrayal, rejection, or loneliness. So, I reached for alcohol, a quick escape from the truth. At first, it was just a drink here and there, a way to take the edge off. The more I drank, the easier it was to pretend I wasn't hurting. It became a routine, a way to silence my thoughts and forget the nights when the walls felt like they were closing in. I blurred the memories of the shattered marriage certificate, the betrayal, and the silence from my loved ones. I'm here to tell you that drowning pain doesn't work, it learns to swim. No matter how much I tried to numb it, it always came back, louder and heavier. One night, it caught up to me.

I was surrounded by people who were lost, broken, and committed to staying in their spiral. Despite this, I knew I had to separate myself. I didn't hate them; I still don't. I love them but realized and extended my prayers to them, hoping they would make the same transformative choice for themselves. Real love is not about confining someone to darkness; it is about releasing them so they may embrace the light when ready.

After my divorce, I believed the worst was over. Walking out barefoot, bleeding, and never looking back seemed the most arduous part. However, leaving a relationship is not solely about achieving freedom; it also entails emptiness, which can be deafening. I was averse to experiencing betrayal, rejection, and loneliness, so I sought solace in alcohol, a fleeting escape from reality. I obscured the memories of the shattered marriage certificate, the betrayal, and the silence from my loved ones.

One fateful night, it caught up with me. The universe was saying, "Enough." I was intoxicated and driving recklessly, which should never have occurred. I was apprehended for driving under the influence (DUI). It was a profound spiritual moment, during which everything came into sharp focus. The universe conveyed a message: "Enough." Sitting there, sober enough to comprehend but intoxicated sufficient to feel the weight of shame, I realized a profound truth: this was not my true self. This was not the version of myself I aspired to embody and carry into my envisioned future. It was not solely alcohol; it was also the realization that I needed to transform.

In a state of quiet withdrawal, I created physical distance to regain control of my thoughts and emotions. This process extended beyond alcohol consumption, encompassing the chaotic environment that had become my norm. Peace felt foreign after enduring dysfunction for an extended period. Facing the pain sober and directly, I gradually cleared the clutter of my mind. What emerged on the other side was not perfection or immediate healing, but clarity. I realized that I no longer needed alcohol or constant companionship to find fulfillment. I was empowered to make choices that prioritized my well-being, even if it meant letting go of familiar routines.

Reflecting on that period, I do not harbor shame for my actions. Instead, I recognize that sometimes complete disintegration is necessary to gain a clear perspective on what truly matters. I was worthy of saving, and so were the individuals I still cherished, albeit from a distance. The DWI served as a wake-up call, stripping me bare and exposing my vulnerabilities.

While the cuffs were not physically restrictive, the emotional burden of shame suffocated me. Sitting in the police car, the flashing lights reflected off the mirror, creating a surreal and impersonal experience like being forced into a role in a movie.

The officers' polite demeanor made the situation even more disconcerting. They were not angry, but I was consumed by self-loathing for allowing my pain to consume me and for trusting someone who ultimately led me to despair. That night did not culminate in incarceration. Instead, it ended in a quiet, frigid room where I found myself stone-cold sober. Lying on the bed, gazing at the ceiling, I felt a profound sense of emptiness. Then, silence descended upon me, not the oppressive silence that instilled fear. This silence was cleansing, revealing the truth. I heard my voice in that stillness, faint, bruised, and uncertain, yet distinctly mine. I recognized the urgency of immediate change to prevent its permanent loss.

Recovery is not a neatly packaged redemption arc. It is messy, painful, and honest. I sought alcohol not for its taste, but for the escape it provided. I missed the absence of intense emotions, the blurring of consciousness, the numbness, and the quiet that soothed the lingering grief when the house was still. However, I remained present, even when it was excruciating. While friends shared pictures from bars, I remained alone on weekends, projecting an image of perfection. I refrained from unfollowing or blocking them, allowing the silence to speak for me. Slowly and painfully, it did. They ceased reaching out because my silence mirrored their chaos. Not everyone is prepared to confront their reality.

Previously, I believed that earning love required constant availability, unwavering affirmation, and the sacrifice of my well-being. Sobriety taught me a different perspective. Love does not necessitate destruction. Genuine love facilitates healing, even if it entails witnessing someone's departure, remaining silent, or grappling with uncertainty about connecting with them.

Unfortunately, some individuals were unable or unwilling to engage in such a relationship. Painfully, I ceased attempting to rescue those not drawn to me. I realized that sobriety was about reclaiming my voice, truth, and future. The bottle had spoken louder than me, but now my voice is more audible. I couldn't stay with them because it would prevent my healing. So, I made the hardest decision: to step away in love. It wasn't easy to accept this truth: caring deeply for someone and still having to step back. You can't save someone who doesn't want to be saved or you yourself heal in an environment that reopens wounds.

Chapter 20
Chosen for Something Greater
"Sometimes your purpose whispers long before you're ready to answer it."

After spiraling into a state of depression, alcoholism, and social isolation, I unexpectedly discovered a therapeutic outlet through writing. Initially, it was a simple act of scribbling, expressing thoughts and feelings that I had been unable to articulate. I would grab a piece of paper and a pen, allowing my emotions to flow freely onto the page. The words felt like a lifeline, releasing the overwhelming emotions swirling within me. While some of my writings were messy, raw, and unplanned, patterns emerged as I continued to write. These patterns formed rhythms that resonated with a poetic quality. One day, I realized that my writing was not just words but lyrics. Not polished or refined, but authentic expressions of heartbreak, survival, and the journey of healing.

For the first time in a long time, I experienced a glimmer of hope. I realized that my soul had been trying to communicate with me: my voice, even imperfect, was destined to reach others. Although I was not fully healed, I recognized this as my calling. I aimed to transform pain, betrayal, and silence into something that could heal and inspire others. It did not matter that I lacked musical knowledge or singing skills; what mattered was that my inner voice refused to be silenced. Each lyric felt like a piece of me awakening, while each off-key melody resonated with solace and connection. As I embraced this newfound passion, the universe encouraged me to continue. While I may not have all the answers, I understood that my presence was not solely for survival. My purpose was to create, heal, and connect with others. Although I was not ready to provide direct assistance, I knew my music would eventually serve that purpose. When that day arrived, my compositions would carry the truth of my life, not for personal gain or recognition, but for those who needed to hear the reassuring message, "You are not alone."

This was not merely a dream but a profound calling that guided me even in the quiet moments of everyday life. Purpose does not manifest in grand gestures or flashing signs; it whispers, nudges, and often presents as an overlooked moment. For me, that moment came on a quiet afternoon in a grocery store parking lot. I was not there to purchase groceries; I was seeking solace and coping with my struggles. In a moment of introspection, I seized a napkin and began writing a sentence that felt like it had been waiting for years: "Perhaps I was not broken; perhaps I was becoming." In that realization, I understood that the pain I perceived as overwhelming was shaping me. It was not destroying me; it was transforming me. I no longer sought labels, record deals, or an audience. All I required was a pen, a voice, and the courage to express my authentic truth. Telling the truth, unadulterated and honest, can shatter people's defenses.

My intuition recognized that if I took the first step, others might find the strength to follow. Discovering one's purpose after experiencing devastation is a sacred journey. I ceased chasing applause and approval and created from a deep, authentic place. The validation of others was secondary to the desire to be heard. It was about the version of myself who persevered despite every reason to succumb. I wept, prayed, and whispered to God, seeking a purpose for my pain. That is the voice I now sing, the weathered, resilient, and transformed version. I have overcome betrayal, heartbreak, and shame, finding a melody beneath the layers of adversity. That is why I continue to write and dream, even when it frightens me. I believe a purpose was planted within me, and each storm I have weathered has nurtured that seed.

When the opportune moment presents itself, it will flourish. Instead of lamenting, "Why did this happen to me?" I pose the question, "How can I transform this situation?" This is not merely a chapter; it is a launching pad. I was selected not because I possessed extraordinary strength or qualifications, but because I was willing. Willing to embrace the vulnerability of experiencing emotions, falling, and expressing my truth, even in its imperfections. Now, I am prepared to rise.

There were moments when I questioned everything, sitting alone with a notebook, contemplating whether this would truly matter. Without an audience, spotlight, or external validation, I was left with myself, my pen, and a whisper in my spirit that urged me to persevere. That whisper became my guiding principle. When reduced to nothingness, devoid of applause, the dissolution of a marriage, the silence of a family, and the numbness of despair, all that remained was the unadulterated truth.

Within that sacred space, I discovered my power not in feigning or attempting to be someone I was not, but in embracing my imperfections, honoring my scars, and acknowledging my pain. My songs were not composed for chart success or awards recognition, but for the young boy who sat alone, contemplating whether he would ever feel seen, and for the adult man who abandoned his home barefoot and bleeding yet chose to embark on a new journey. They were written for every soul who inquired, "Will my pain ever hold significance?" My response is affirmative. Each lyric, melody, and note is a component of my healing, resonating through the silence that once consumed me.

A larger stage awaits, not merely for my performance, but for me to share my survival, grace, and the realization that sometimes the overlooked are bestowed with the deepest anointing. Fear of obscurity no longer holds me captive, for I am cognizant that authenticity never remains concealed. When my moment arrives, I will not perform a role but respond to a divine call. Although my purpose may not be universally understood, I am determined to acquire the knowledge I am destined to possess. I will embrace the stage life that presents itself to me, not as someone fortunate, but as someone destined for greatness.

A profound silence descends before dawn, before the light illuminates the horizon and the world recognizes your name. I am currently immersed in this sacred hush. It is not a glamorous existence. It is devoid of dazzling stage lights and adoring fans. It comprises quiet mornings, unfinished lyrics, and moments when doubt attempts to masquerade as logic. However, I have come to recognize that voice, the one that challenges my self-worth, and respond with truth: I am someone who has endured hardship and emerged victorious. That is sufficient.

My artistry is not built on hype or fleeting trends. The essence of real-life nurtures it, the depths of grief and joy, the losses and awakenings, and the ashes of what I once believed I needed, revealing the clarity of my true essence. With each return to the page, the melody, and the mirror, I emerge with a new version of myself, a more healed, authentic, and aligned individual. I once believed that I needed to attain a certain level of achievement before I could be worthy of being heard. However, I have realized that true worth lies not in perfection, but in presence. My voice does not need to conform to others' norms, my songs do not need to follow a predetermined formula, and my story does not need to be neatly structured to be transformative. All that matters is that it is authentic to me. Thus, I am becoming the kind of artist I was always meant to be, not one shaped by external pressures, but one molded by my purpose. I sing not because I am fearless, but because I recall the profound silence that once enveloped me, waiting for a voice that resonated with its essence. Therefore, if it is my destiny to be the one to write it, I will.

If it is my destiny to face the challenges head-on, I will. If it is my destiny to create songs that transcend conventional boundaries and touch the souls of those who listen, I will. My mission has never been mass approval. It has always been impact, connection, and leaving behind a legacy of healing so profound that even after my passing, someone may encounter one of my lyrics and find the strength to persevere through their struggles. That is the kind of artist I aspire to become, not one who seeks excessive attention or perfection but who remains steadfast and authentic. I refuse to be paralyzed by waiting for the perfect moment to act; I choose to move forward with purpose and conviction.

If I am remembered for anything, let it not be the polished sound of my voice or the extent of my success, but for the unwavering truth I choose to express in a world that often prioritizes superficiality. Because I lived life without refusing to succumb to despair and sing with raw emotion, authenticity, and redemption. That, my friends, has always been the essence of my artistry.

Chapter 21
A Stage Meant for Healing
"Some dreams aren't about being seen-they're about making others feel seen."

*I*nitially, my writing was a personal outlet for survival and emotional expression. However, as I poured my feelings onto paper, I realized that my lyrics transcended my individual experiences. They resonated with the feelings of anyone who had ever been silenced, rejected, or doubted their worth. This realization sparked a profound understanding: my music had the potential to serve as a mirror for healing and self-discovery. I envisioned my lyrics being sung by individuals in the crowd, strangers who, through my words, found a respite for their own life and misdoings. The stage, the lights, and the power of music became symbols of unity and a reminder that they were not alone.

In that vision, I experienced a sense of purpose that had eluded me for a long time. Fame and celebrity status were not my motivations; instead, I sought to use my platform to reach those who felt invisible and sat in silence with their pain, just as I once did. I envisioned standing on that stage and letting my voice convey a message of hope and reassurance:

"You are not forgotten. You are not beyond repair. You still matter."

The prospect of achieving global fame did not intimidate me but humbled me. I recognized that my music would resonate with me and the countless individuals who had faced similar struggles. There would be the boy left out of the Christmas picture, the boy blamed for the actions of others, the young man beaten for attempting escape, and the husband who walked out barefoot and bleeding. All these versions of myself would be standing there, finally free.

While I acknowledge that I am not yet fully prepared, I know the clear calling that guides me. I recognize the need to continue learning and growing as a singer, musician, and as an individual. However, the purpose I have discovered is undeniable, and I am determined to fulfill it. This was not merely a dream or escape but my destiny. Even during moments of self-doubt, my spirit persisted, whispering, "This is greater than you. Persevere."

Thus, I continued to write, dream, and envision that stage, not for applause or recognition, but for the moment when someone in the audience would finally experience the healing I had long sought: The transformative power of music. It transcends mere sound, reaching where words alone falter. It mends the wounds we believed beyond repair. If my story, my voice, could evoke such healing in even one soul, it would all be worthwhile. Though I am not yet there, I am certain I will one day step onto that stage. When I do, I will recognize that it was not solely for me but for all of us. When our younger selves are denied the opportunity to be heard, an enduring ache lingers.

When I envision the stage, I do not merely see lights, music, and applause; I expect a reunion, a spiritual reckoning, and a sacred moment where the silenced parts of others finally find their voice. I imagine gazing out at the crowd and seeing not just strangers, but reflections of myself, people who were dismissed, overlooked, or discarded holding their breath because somehow, my voice echoes their unspoken words. In that realization, I understood that my trials, the abandonment, the humiliation, the spiritual warnings, the violence, the loss were not meant to destroy me; they were meant to prepare me.

To become a voice for those still lost in the darkness. Hold the microphone for the boy excluded from the Christmas drawing, to sing for the child who found solace in a culvert, escaping the absurdity of their world. The voice that would testify for the man who fled a house bleeding, not just physically, but emotionally shattered. These are not mere scenes in a memoir; they are tangible evidence of survival. I carry every one of them with me to that stage. For that is what makes the message authentic. In essence, healing does not render flawless but fosters transparency.

I will refrain from feigning perfection when I finally stand under those lights. Instead, I will embody a proven individual who has endured adversity and refrained from harming others in return. This is the trajectory I am aspiring to achieve; an artist grounded in presence rather than performance. If a single individual emerges from a show feeling lighter, stronger, and more understood, my mission will have been accomplished. It was never solely about my voice being heard. It was always about fostering a sense of wholeness in others.

I have envisioned this moment in countless ways. Perhaps in a dimly lit room, the audience holds its breath. The lights gradually get dim, and the atmosphere shifts and just before the first note resonates, there is an unwavering stillness. Not fear nor nerves, but reverence fills the air. In that moment, deep within my core, I will recognize the profound purpose of every detour. Not validation nor fame, but the culmination. That sacred instant when pain intertwines with purpose, and I finally deliver the message that has resided within me for decades: "You have overcome adversity. You are safe now, and you were never insane for experiencing profound emotions."

That initial note will carry the weight of my past, not to re-traumatize, but to transform. It will catalyze healing, demonstrating that even the most fragmented fragments of our narratives can become instruments of solace when we possess the courage to unveil them. I will not step onto that stage to perform; instead, I will embark on a journey to liberate individuals, and I will accomplish this through rhythm, soul, and authentic lyrics.

Amidst that crowd, someone will clutch their seat, suppressing tears, for they will recognize their own life reflected in my voice. When the performance concludes, I will not seek applause. Instead, I will seek out the faces that have undergone transformation, the burdens that have been lifted, and the eyes that have finally found solace in kindness. In that moment, I will comprehend that my journey has transcended mere artistic pursuit.

It has become a bridge, connecting pain and empowerment, isolation and intimacy, and silence. Initially, my writing served as a personal outlet for survival and emotional expression. However, as I poured my feelings onto paper, I realized that my lyrics transcended my individual experiences. They resonated with the feelings of anyone who had ever been silenced, rejected, or doubted their worth. This realization sparked a profound understanding: my music had the potential to serve as a mirror for healing and self-discovery. I envisioned my lyrics being sung by individuals in the crowd, strangers

144

who through my words, found peace and connection. The stage, the lights, and the power of music became symbols of unity and a reminder that they were not alone.

There's a sacredness in a crown that transcends its symbolic status, becoming a bridge that connects disparate elements: pain and empowerment, isolation and intimacy, silence and sound. Perhaps it serves not solely as a symbol of status but as a signal of survival against intended destruction.

Empowered, I now embark on a journey, reclaiming my identity without seeking permission. My debut performance of Velvet Flex will not merely mark a commencement, but rather a reckoning. By then, the world will be familiar with my backstory, the quiet boy who wept on Christmas Eve, the man who walked barefoot from a life shattered, and the writer who poured truth onto the page. They will witness the voice that refused to succumb. When the track finally drops, smooth, rich, and evocative, it will transcend the realm of music and become a tangible memory.

Velvet curtains will flicker behind, creating a mesmerizing ambiance. The beat will pulse like a heartbeat, echoing the resilience of survival. Rather than strutting out, I will glide with calm and purpose. Wearing the crown is not a display of vanity, but a reminder that survival and brilliance coexist. Individuals who doubted their worth will begin to move from the back row. It may start with a gentle toe tap, followed by a nod, and eventually, a full-blown dance that defies their exhaustion. That moment will mark the success of my mission. It will demonstrate that genre, charts, and gatekeepers hold no sway.

Velvet Flex's essence lies in its vibration, which reclaims the rhythm lost during periods of overwhelming stress. When I sing the lyric, "We used to move as one," I am not merely referring to dance; I am conveying the message of healing, collective return, and sacred rebellion disguised as celebration. Velvet Flex transcends the boundaries of a mere song; it is a spiritual awakening, a homecoming, and a manifestation of freedom. I will exhale as the final note reverberates through the room, releasing a profound sense of liberation. The boy who once sang into pillows, afraid to be heard, has now electrified stadiums with sacred sound.

Chapter 22

Becoming the Vessel

"Sometimes the weight you're carrying isn't yours-it's the people you were never meant to take with you."

$\mathcal{E}$mbracing your purpose is a journey of letting go and the allure of fulfilling one's purpose and that right there is captivating. However, it is crucial to recognize that the initial step is not about adding new elements but about releasing expectations and embracing reality. I once believed that specific individuals would remain in my life indefinitely. These friends shared laughter, trust, and an unwavering conviction that they would support me through life's challenges. However, as the tumultuous events of my life unfolded, divorce, spiraling depression, and alcoholism began to perceive these individuals for their true nature.

Some individuals withdrew quietly, while others betrayed me with unwavering audacity. Others remained only long enough to serve their interests and left me disillusioned. This realization extended beyond friendships; it encompassed my family. The same family whose silence and rejection had already deeply wounded me. Despite the fragile thread of hope that they might change, every interaction served as a stark reminder of their inability to meet my needs.

The struggle to reconcile this realization with betraying oneself when choosing to distance oneself from family was intense. However, the constant cycle of emotional distress and the gradual deterioration of my well-being made it increasingly evident that remaining in this toxic environment was detrimental to my healing process.

The pivotal moment came when I reached a quiet acceptance: I realized that my family would never provide me with the love and support I craved. Holding on to them was perpetuating the pain I sought to overcome. I made the most challenging decision with profound determination: I released them from my life. This included my parents, my brothers, and the individuals who had given me life but had never offered the kind of love that truly made life worthwhile.

On the night of this decision, I found peace within my car, listening to Kesha's "Praying." As the lyrics resonated through the speakers, I experienced a profound connection with the song, as if my soul was responding to the emotions expressed. The lyrics deeply resonated with my experiences: the pain, the release, and the complex mix of anger, sadness, and freedom intertwined within me. As she sang, "I can thank you for how strong I have become," the line resonated profoundly, acknowledging the truth's twisted nature.

Their rejection, betrayal, and silence had all compelled me to discover strength within myself that I was previously unaware of. As the song climaxed, I found myself in tears, not out of a desire for reconciliation, but as a release of the weight of letting go. Hate did not consume me, nor did I harbor any ill feelings. However, I recognized that maintaining connections with them would hinder my healing, prevent my liberation, and hinder my fulfillment of my true purpose.

This realization extended beyond family ties; it encompassed every toxic relationship, every friendship built on convenience rather than genuine care, and every individual who had shown love only when I was functional, silent, or compliant. These individuals could not accompany me on my journey. The loss was profound, and there were nights when I wept for the loved ones I had to release. There were moments when I yearned to reach back, mend the brokenness, and cling to the familiar. Yet, deep within me, I understood that some people are meant to be in our lives for a specific season, not a lifetime. Holding onto them beyond their season would only stifle the growth and purpose meant to flourish.

Therefore, I embarked on a journey of clearing space, creating a sanctuary for peace, clarity, and the version of myself being called to a higher purpose. This did not imply a cessation of my care or love for them. I still cherished them and held hope for their healing. However, I could not simultaneously carry their pain and my own. This pivotal moment marked the commencement of my metamorphosis into the embodiment of my destined purpose, transcending the limitations of music and healing. The weight of my past hindered my ability to fulfill this higher calling.

Releasing the past is not a sign of weakness but a testament to wisdom. It acknowledges that sometimes, the most compassionate act for oneself and others is to create distance, allowing both souls to breathe and find healing. I did not abandon them due to a waning love; I embraced self-love and embarked on self-discovery and fulfillment. I embarked on a transformative odyssey at that juncture, becoming the conduit for a transcendent purpose. When the term "chosen" is invoked, it often evokes images of light and illumination. However, the path to fulfillment does not invariably entail the immediate acquisition of a microphone or the adoration of an audience. Occasionally, it necessitates the initial burden of pain, loneliness, and isolation. This period of self-deprivation often entails shedding false identities and societal expectations, leading to profound self-reflection and introspection.

Before my ascension as the vessel, I underwent a cleansing process, shedding illusions, attachments, and the masks I wore to seek acceptance from superficial individuals who favored a diminished version of myself. Initially, this emptiness felt like abandonment, punishment, and the dissolution of all that held me together. However, it was not a harbinger of destruction but a catalyst for rebuilding. Amidst the silence that ensued when my phone ceased ringing and the individuals I had relied upon failed to respond, a profound transformation transpired. I stopped waiting and ceased to implore for validation. Instead, I redirected my attention to my inner voice, intuition, and a higher power.

Through this transformative process, I realized that being left alone was not a curse but a divine intervention, clearing the path for the authentic essence to manifest. In essence, I was not merely losing individuals but also shedding the need for external validation. I was breaking the habit of settling for less than I deserved. I was releasing relationships that had subtly taught me that love depended on my efforts to earn it. Finally, I grasped the truth that love was not a commodity to be acquired but a divine gift.

I no longer felt compelled to prove my worth through excessive exertion or silence to maintain peace. Instead, a gradual shift occurred, and I began to feel a sense of lightness. This transformation did not diminish my pain but freed me from its grasp, allowing me to hold it with greater clarity and compassion. My hands no longer clung to fleeting moments or unattainable desires. Instead, they remained open, receptive to the divine presence that sought to fill my life. Intriguingly, the healing process often does not manifest as conventional healing. Sometimes, it can feel like an extended period of loneliness, albeit in a state of illumination. One does not suddenly awaken, surrounded by individuals who comprehend and support them. Instead, they remain alone, yet their inner clarity and tranquility deepen. The desperation for external validation dissipates, replaced by a profound sense of inner peace. In that hushed moment, I experienced a profound sense of peace I had not felt in years.

This peace did not stem from an easier life. Instead, it arose from a cessation of my constant pleas for the storm to subside and a newfound ability to construct shelter within its midst. I ceased performing, ceased explaining, and ceased chasing. For the first time, I began to embody a version of myself that I genuinely respected. This was not the perpetual availability, perpetual agreeableness, and perpetual fear of disappointing version of myself. Instead, it was the version that could endure discomfort without resorting to escape. It was the version that could assert its boundaries, choose itself, and prioritize its well-being. This version lacked ostentation and did not seek admiration or belonging. It simply recognized its inherent worth and the veracity of its existence. This transformation made me the receptacle for this newfound peace. I was not flawless, but I had finally attained a wholeness that enabled me to emanate from a place of authenticity. Not everyone perceived this change. Some labeled it selfish and cold. However, I refrained from explaining, for what they perceived as "changing" was my journey of self-discovery and self-acceptance.

I could no longer endure the burden of their misunderstandings. I had a purpose to fulfill, a genuine purpose that transcended fame and praise. My objective was to align myself with my authentic self and enter the world with open hands, a mended heart, and a voice that carried more than mere sound, it possessed substance.

This kind of vessel did not seek permission; it commenced pouring forth its essence. As I cleared the clutter of what was not meant for me, I created space for the meaningful opportunities that sought to enter my life. These opportunities did not arrive abruptly; they arrived gradually, subtly communicating their presence to me through messages, song ideas, and the touch of strangers who found solace in my narrative. These were not mere coincidences; they were affirmations. They demonstrated that when one aligns with their purpose, the universe conspires almost in an orchestrated manner. Alignment does not guarantee ease; it demands perseverance, unwavering trust in the vision before the evidence manifests, and the courage to rise and work even when no one applauds. Even when the room remains empty, doubt creeps in like fog at 3 a.m., questioning my sanity for believing in the potential of such a profound impact originating from someone like me. However, I did not construct this for external validation. I embarked on this journey because I had no alternative.

The call persisted, refusing to allow me to escape. The pain I endured held significance. If I could channel that pain into illuminating even a single candle in someone else's darkness, none of it would be in vain. Becoming the vessel was not driven by fame; it was rooted in faith. It entailed the willingness to carry the essence of healing, creativity, and truth without compromising it to please individuals who were never destined to hold the cup. I recognized that my voice was not solely mine but borrowed from a sacred source. Would dishonoring that voice by succumbing to shrinking, performing, or pretending constitute the ultimate betrayal? Therefore, I persevere, even on challenging days. Even when the lingering grief attempts to haunt me. When the silence extends beyond my comfort zone, I have come to understand: The vessel does not need to be flawless; it merely needs to be willing to serve, and I am.

I proceed forward, radiating a sense of lightness, clarity, and liberation. This transformation does not stem from achieving a comprehensive understanding of the future. Instead, it arises from ceasing to carry burdens that were never mine to bear. While I may not have a clear path ahead, I am sure of this: I have transcended the pursuit of belonging and become the embodiment of belonging. In assuming the role of the vessel, I have found peace in letting go, as it has created space for the arrival of everything sacred that is destined to come.

Chapter 23

The Cleansing Before the Rise

*"Before the universe gives you more, it asks
you to make room."*

An unexpected transformation occurred after
an emotionally charged farewell, estrangement from
my family, and gradual distance from friends. Initially
unsettling, the silence became a sanctuary. For the
first time, I had ample space to breathe, think
without judgment, feel without interference, and
confront suppressed questions. I commenced by
waking up with a sense of calm instead of dread,
listening to my thoughts instead of running away,
and prioritizing peace and tranquility. This cleansing
extended beyond physical well-being, impacting my
emotions and spirit. I became discerning in selecting
individuals and energies, choosing words that
resonated with my soul, and treating my peace as a
sacred entity. In this quietude, clarity emerged. I
gained insight into the influence of survival on my
life, how I had primarily reacted to pain rather than
creating from it. Now, I was alone, free from
distractions hindering self-discovery. Antiquated
habits dissipated. Alcohol's allure diminished, toxic
conversations lost appeal, and chaos no longer felt
like a sanctuary. Peace permeated my life, quiet yet
profound, enabling me to hear my soul's whispers
finally.

This period marked the cusp before the ascent, when I was not yet prepared to perform, fully healed, or fully equipped to confront the world. In contrast, I diligently cleared the path. For the first time, that felt sufficient. I commenced dreaming with purpose. I envisioned composing more music, strengthening my vocal cords, and singing for those in need. I recognized that my efforts were preparing me for a cleansing process. Occasionally, I missed those I had distanced myself from and doubted my decision. However, when I found peace, I received a gentle whisper: "Trust this. You are creating space for greater fulfillment." Through perseverance, I shed purging habits, emotional baggage, and pain.

Gradually, I felt lighter, not because the past vanished, but because I no longer carried its weight. This was the season of renewal, the juncture before breakthrough, the cleansing before ascent. The silence was not merely a respite; it was a metamorphosis. Without external expectations, I discovered my authentic needs: rest, truth, and the freedom to breathe without guilt. Above all, I yearned for the deity I had always sensed, who accompanied me in my darkest moments and transcended church buildings to communicate through silence. Thus, I began seeking Him in hushed moments, early morning light, and journal entries that transformed into prayers. During extended drives without a destination, with worship music playing, I refrained from imploring God to rectify the situation. Instead, I invited Him to be present. This in itself proved more therapeutic than my fervent pleas. I realized I did not need more possessions; I needed fewer significant items. I relinquished the need for productivity and to prove my worthiness of love, and I released uncontrollable timelines.

In this act of letting go, I rebuilt. It was not aesthetically pleasing, but it resonated with inner fulfillment. This period of transformation was my wilderness season, not barren, but a sanctuary of growth and blossoming, a sacred in-between space between my past self and my evolving identity.

I understood that the universe was purging me because a larger, more transformative force was attempting to manifest. I had mistakenly believed that "becoming" was an abrupt and dramatic process, but my experience was gradual and sacred, unfolding quietly in stillness. It was not an overnight transformation but a moment-by-moment, choice-by-choice process.

This transformation enabled me to assert my boundaries without guilt, cease explaining myself to misinterpret, and recognize my boundaries as sacred gates to a holy realm because they were. This transformation was not about isolation; it was about protection. I was not severing myself from the world but safeguarding my emerging self. Healing has an unacknowledged facet: genuine transformation. For instance, deleting numbers from my phone, resisting a bottle in the store, or refraining from letting a memory derail my day, these represent healing, growth, and transformation. They were not dramatic; they were intentional.

Previously, I sought escape; now, I pray for alignment. I no longer yearned for pain to disappear; I aspire to uncover its purpose. I have grasped the profound understanding that every ending conceals a new beginning, every loss creates space for something sacred, and every silence nurtures my future's flourishing. This cleansing was not punishment; it was preparation. I was not abandoned; I was anointed. The version of myself that yearned for love, validation, or tolerance has vanished. What remains is an individual who understands the cost of peace and is willing to pay it. I am not hardened; I am clear about my identity, burdens, and lost opportunities. Establishing one's sanctuary is profoundly sanctifying. One no longer relies on external rescue, outsources worth, or conveys pain to those who do not understand. This cleansing was the quiet transition.

For the first time, I am ready for the unfolding chapter. The rise will not be noisy; it will be confirmed. At the right time, with the right people, and on the right stage. Not for attention; for alignment. What is coming is not about fame; it is about fulfillment. I am entering the next chapter, not just as a participant, but as an ascendant. This time, I carried nothing that was not destined to accompany me. Somewhere along the way, I ceased asking,

"Why did this happen to me?" ...
and commenced asking, ...
"What is this preparing me for?"

The silence was not punishment. It was a sacred preparation. Every goodbye, every breakdown, every unanswered prayer. It was not the end; it was clearing the runway. It is impossible to rise above the burdens of the past.

Carrying one's purpose while entangled in the weight of one's former self is an insurmountable challenge. Therefore, I decided to release all that held me back. The noise, the guilt, and the relentless pressure to prove myself to others vanished. In their place remained a vessel, not empty, but prepared. The readiness I possess does not demand attention or declaration. It is simply a state of being, a presence that arrives unannounced, different, focused, and anointed. When they witness my ascent, let them believe it occurred overnight. Let them assume it was a matter of chance. Let them ponder

160

how I managed to remain grounded while embarking on this journey of flight. For those who truly comprehend, they will understand: The cleansing that preceded my rise made the flight possible.

I once believed the breakthrough would come with a grand spectacle, a moment of undeniable change. However, true healing, the kind that transforms lives, arrived like a whisper. It came when no one was watching, when I ceased performing and began listening. It came when I extended grace to myself instead of succumbing to grief. I ceased waiting for closure from those who were incapable of providing it. I ceased rereading old wounds as if they held new answers and I ceased attempting to mend broken connections that God had already released.

The rise is not about ascending higher but shedding the weight that held me down. Now, I do not see the same person when I gaze upon my reflection. Not because I have undergone a complete transformation, but because I have finally begun to honor the sacred essence of who I am. Peace has become my guiding principle, not attention, approval, or any fleeting sense of validation. From this profound peace, I embarked on the construction of something sacred.

This chapter of my life may never be loud, trendy, or widely recognized, but it will forever hold a place in my memory. It was here, amidst the quiet and the cleansing, that I rediscovered my true self and more importantly, I rediscovered who I was becoming.

Chapter 24
Preparing for the Stage
"When you're ready to take the first step, the right teacher always appears. But not all teachers are meant to stay."

$\mathcal{F}$ollowing the cleansing, the period of tranquility, and the decision to create space for my healing, I experienced an inexplicable pull toward a new endeavor. I recognized that merely dreaming about the stage would no longer suffice. If I genuinely aspired to heal through music, not solely for my own sake, but also for the benefit of others, I would require initiating the necessary preparations. This entailed learning, personal growth, and aligning my soul with my vision.

During this transformative period, I encountered an individual who seemed to appear at the opportune moment. This person served as a mentor, not merely as a vocal coach, but someone with extensive experience in the music industry. Their connections extended to renowned artists, including Dr. Dre, granting them a profound understanding of music's business and artistic aspects. Moreover, they comprehended the profound spiritual significance of becoming an artist with a message. Meeting this individual did not feel like a coincidence; it resonated with a sense of alignment. It was as if the universe was affirming my seriousness and offering guidance on navigating the challenges ahead.

During our initial session, I could sense a profound shift in dynamics. This vocal training deviated from the conventional "do-re-me" approach. The coach did not merely perceive my voice as a flaw to be corrected; instead, they delved into the essence of my soul behind it. While they did not indulge in coddling, they compelled me to confront my voice honestly. They identified my areas of weakness while simultaneously highlighting my strengths, where the emotions and truths resided. Their focus extended beyond pitch and tone, delving into the concept of energy. They elucidated that the voice is an instrument and a mirror of the soul. They imparted profound wisdom, "If you are not internally aligned, your music will never resonate with external audiences." This statement left an indelible mark on my consciousness. Our sessions did not adhere to a rigid schedule. On certain days, we engaged in vocal warm-ups and breathing exercises.

On other days, we embarked on extended conversations that explored various aspects of life, including pain and the intricacies of the music industry. It dawned on me that these sessions transcended mere vocal training; they constituted artist development. They were shaping me into more than just a singer, molding me into a vessel capable of carrying a profound message. Everything seemed to fall into place for a period, and I experienced a sense of unwavering progress. I pursued my musical aspirations and engaged in various activities, including lyric writing, guitar practice, and melody creation. I recorded these sessions as audio messages to share with him, expressing my vulnerability and seeking guidance. However, a shift occurred, and the responses I received diminished. The energy in our interactions changed, and he became increasingly silent. When I finally communicated with him, he provided an excuse citing a heavy workload with numerous clients. Despite his scheduled lessons and notifications, I never received them.

This divergence in our paths left me questioning my worthiness, the appropriateness of my requests, and any potential errors on my part. However, I recognized that this situation was not solely about me. It reflected the inherent nature of his role in my life. After some reflection, I realized he was not destined to accompany me on this journey. His presence was limited to a specific season, a period that provided me with a catalyst, inspiration, and guidance. He served as a steppingstone, enabling me to envision my potential and take the necessary steps.

Accepting this truth brought me a sense of gratitude and released me from resentment and dwelling on the silence. I embraced the lessons, inspiration, and reminder that this journey was mine to own. During my musical journey, his season fulfilled its intended purpose: it ignited a spark within me, provided a glimpse of my potential, and motivated me to persevere even when the path became uncertain. As I embarked on my journey again, I gained a profound realization: even transient connections can have a transformative impact. They are not about permanence; they are about purpose.

Driven by this newfound understanding, I continued to practice and pursue my musical aspirations. I retained the vision of the stage in my mind, recognizing that the appropriate mentors and guides would arrive at the opportune moments.

I also understood that sometimes, these individuals are only meant to remain for a brief period to unlock the next phase of my development.

I was not yet there, but I was closer. That was sufficient.

Previously, I believed that someone else had to guide me to my destination. I sought permission, validation, and a gatekeeper. However, when his silence became permanent, I ceased waiting. I stopped waiting to be chosen, guided, or discovered. Instead, I took responsibility for my journey. I realized genuine preparation does not involve relying on someone else to hold my hand. It is about developing the ability to listen to my inner voice more effectively than the noise of others. I recalled his words:

"If you are not internally aligned, your music will never resonate externally."

I abandoned the pursuit of perfection. Instead, I focused on alignment. This entailed performing the necessary work that others may not perceive. The vocal exercises were conducted in solitude. The songwriting sessions were with only my soul as an audience. The quiet conviction in myself when no one was applauding. I began to manifest as the artist I envisioned, even if my voice faltered, the melodies were imperfect, and my content did not garner any responses. I persisted. Because preparation is not glamorous, it is arduous. No stage, regardless of its brilliance, can sustain a soul that has not been fortified in the shadows. In embracing solitude, I realized that divine timing is not delayed but meticulously orchestrated. An individual's departure from a narrative does not imply its conclusion. Perhaps my purpose was to learn how to lead myself. Maybe the mentor's silence was the lesson.

Consequently, I trained as if the stage were imminent. I rehearsed as if the audience were already present. I healed as if the spotlight depended on it. Because if I were to present the notion that healing is attainable to the world, I would first have to embody that concept. Even when no one was observing, even when my initial collaborators moved on, especially during that period, that is when the artist emerges.

Every artist yearns for the stage. However, not every artist prepares for the weight that comes with it. I posed a question to myself: Was I constructing something sacred? Or merely seeking applause? Because the spotlight does not provide solace, it exposes one's vulnerabilities. I refrained from shedding blood on stage from wounds I had not addressed in private.

I made a solemn vow to myself: The version of me that touches that microphone will be complete. Or at the very least, candid about the ongoing healing process. Discipline became my new mentor. It was not glamorous; it resembled vocal exercises when I was fatigued. Revisions when I believed the song was finalized. Warm-ups in the car, in the shower, even on days when I lacked the inclination to sing. Each time I adhered to my commitment, I evolved into a more authentic version of myself. The absence of applause and social media recognition did not hinder my progress. However, I could sense a palpable transformation.

My lungs grew stronger, my melodies became more fluid, and my presence became more grounded. I was shedding the version of myself that awaited discovery and embracing the one who recognized his growth potential. Fame was not my objective. I focused on faithfulness to the gift, the message, and my inner vow to the boy who once felt invisible. Upon emerging from this challenging phase, we will also endeavor to assist others in experiencing a sense of visibility.

The young boy was now observing me, and I resolved not to disappoint him. As I prepared my voice, I realized it transcended merely sound, encompassing frequency and alignment and embodying the stage before my performance. When carrying a message, one's life must resonate with greater force than their lyrics. Individuals can discern authenticity when it is genuine, recognizing when a voice is supported by wisdom gained from past experiences, rather than perpetuating silence and wounds. I ceased questioning my talent and instead focused on grounding myself. An inflated sense of self-importance did not drive this, but by a steadfast pursuit of purpose.

When one's purpose is sufficiently strong, rejection does not deter, gradual progress is not faltered, and applause is not sought as validation. Instead, one becomes the source of applause; one's presence precedes them, one's narrative sustains them, and one's healing transforms into an unwavering microphone.

I grasped a previously unfamiliar concept: preparation serves as the platform, the tranquility, the nights of self-doubt, and the moments of breakthrough that occur without external observation. These were the authentic stages, and if I honored these spaces, regardless of the size of the audience, I would cease performing and transition into ministering. Therefore, I ceased seeking permission and waiting for ideal vocal ranges, opportunities, or perfect stages.

Healing imparted a profound lesson: you do not await discovery; you acknowledge your divine purpose. Those destined for greatness do not pursue stages; they embody them, radiate their light into the room, infuse silence with life, and transform pain into melody. Transforming the melody into movement, the training extended beyond mastering vocal techniques. It encompassed learning how to stand tall, breathe through fear, persevere despite obstacles, and hold a microphone with reverence, recognizing its sacred significance. Not for external validation, but for those who remain in darkness, who require a voice to reassure them: "You are not alone. You are not beyond repair. And your narrative is far from concluded."

I have yet to step onto that stage physically, my spirit is already there. And when that moment arrives, I will approach the microphone not as someone preparing for a performance, but as an individual who has already achieved that state.

Chapter 25
Finding My True Voice
*"Your voice doesn't become real when
someone else approves it- it becomes real when
you finally believe it yourself."*

$\mathcal{F}$ollowing the silence from my mentor, I was
faced with a choice: I could allow his absence to
make me question my worth or I could let it
motivate me to stand on my own. I chose the latter.
It felt strange! There was no one to share my
melodies with. No one would provide feedback or
suggest alternative approaches. It was just me and
the voice I was uncertain about trusting. However, as
I embraced this solitude, I realized a profound truth:
Perhaps this was the intended purpose. Maybe I was
not meant to rely on external validation to define my
artistic identity. Perhaps I was destined to discover
my true self through self-discovery.

I embarked on a gradual journey. I picked up
my guitar and played the same chords repeatedly
until they became familiar and comfortable. I
composed lyrics without worrying about their
perceived quality. I began singing softly, gradually
increasing the volume, allowing myself to make
mistakes and embrace imperfection.

In these moments of vulnerability, I discovered
something genuine. It was not polished or flawless,
but it was authentic and raw. It was the same voice
that had been silenced as a child, the same voice that

had been rejected and subjected to abuse. Yet, it was finally speaking not merely through words or melodies, but through the depths of my being. I realized that discovering my musical voice was intrinsically linked to finding my inner voice. They were inseparable. True power lies not in suppressing one's authentic self, but in embracing it and the ability to convey a profound message to the world requires confronting one's fears and vulnerabilities. Consequently, I intertwined the healing power of music with my journey. With each lyric I sang about pain, I released it into the world. I shared a piece of my story with each melody I played without uttering a single word. Slowly but surely, the fear began to dissipate. I ceased pursuing perfection, recognizing that people connect with genuine voices, not flawless ones. The voices that vibrate slightly on high notes. The voices that convey emotion in imperfections. The ones that evoke emotions, even if they are imperfect.

For the first time, I ceased asking, "Is this adequate?" Instead, I began inquiring, "Does this resonate with me?" If it resonated, it was accurate. Authenticity cannot be faked. I also ceased awaiting external validation to determine my belonging. The truth is, I have always belonged. I merely needed to acknowledge it. Discovering my voice was not solely about mastering singing; it was about reclaiming the silenced aspect of myself. The element that was labeled an accident.

The element that was told to me would never be sufficient. The aspect that was instructed to remain subdued and diminutive. That voice is now absent. A new one is emerging. I continue to learn. There are days when I falter, when the lingering doubts resurface. However, I now possess this knowledge: My voice transcends merely as my own lived life narrative for others, healing, and the bridge connect me with the individuals I will reach. Therefore, I persist in singing, even when it is uncertain.

Even when no one is present, each note represents a step closer to my authentic self. Each word carries a truth that someone, somewhere, requires to hear. This is the essence of discovering one's authentic voice. It entails refraining from seeking permission or validation. It involves simply allowing it to emerge.

A peculiar form of liberation emerges when no one is observing. Absence of an audience. Absence of critics. Absence of cheerleaders. Presence of one's raw, unadulterated essence in a secluded room with one's aspirations. That is where I rediscovered my voice, not in a recording studio. In the absence of a stage or a feedback loop of external opinions, I found solace in a moment of tranquility, free from the need for impressiveness. I realized that I had squandered a significant portion of my life seeking external affirmation, neglecting the power of self-affirmation. Consequently, I began treating my voice as a neglected friend, listening to and nurturing it.

Despite repeated failures and moments of silence, I found comfort in the realization that my voice had not failed me. It had patiently awaited my trust. Occasionally, I recorded myself to listen back, not to criticize but to acknowledge the honesty in my voice. I would hear courage in my own imperfections. There were moments when I would become emotional listening to my voice, not because it sounded exceptional, but because it felt liberating. It was free from comparison, shame, and the need to conform to anyone else's expectations.

Surprisingly, as I released my pursuit of "sounding good," I discovered a newfound power in my voice. It was not ostentatious but grounded and rooted in truth. It seemed that the more I honored my story, the more my voice responded in kind.

This revelation led me to embrace a belief that had previously eluded me: that my voice was destined for more than silence. It was not broken, late, or excessive; it was simply waiting for me to cease hiding. I believed that confidence derived from external validation, such as applause or compliments. However, true confidence arises from confronting fear, performing alone, and persevering despite challenges. On nights when I sang with a lump in my throat and tears in my eyes, my voice was not just music; it was a vehicle for carrying the weight of a child who had been labeled as too sensitive, too emotional, too loud, too peculiar, and too much. That child has become the artist, and the qualities once considered flaws have become the essence of the music. The sensitivity, emotion, depth, and fire make my music truly magical.

Instead of measuring success by perfection, I have shifted my focus to authenticity. I ask myself, "Did I sing from a genuine place?" "Did I convey the story honestly?" "Did I allow the pain to speak and the healing to respond?" If the answers are affirmative, I consider it a victory, regardless of whether anyone claps or notices. Even if I were the sole individual who perceived it,

Acknowledging that the most significant individual who requires your voice is yourself is crucial. Once you genuinely hear it, you cannot unhear it. You cannot return to silence, shrink, or diminish yourself for spaces never destined to accommodate your light. I used to question whether I possessed anything worthwhile to express. I doubted the significance of my narrative, the relevance of my pain, and the possibility of my voice being deemed too unconventional, raw, or broken to be received.

I have realized that individuals do not require a flawless voice; they need an authentic one. They do not seek flawless notes; they seek someone who has experienced their emotions and dares to articulate them. This is me. Every scar I bear carries a song within it. Every moment I have survived now bears its melody. I no longer harbor fear of being perceived. For I have already endured the invisibility of silence. The voice I have discovered transcends its individuality and becomes shared.

It resonates with children contemplating their worthiness of being heard, adults concealing behind smiles, apprehensive that their truth may jeopardize everything, and individuals who have been advised to remain small, silent, and safe. To them, I proclaim: Utilize your voice regardless of its tremors, initial quietude, or the absence of applause. For the moment you utter your truth, you liberate yourself from the constraints of your past. You become a beacon of inspiration for another. The trajectory of this journey remains uncertain. I am sure of this: I have discovered my voice, and I shall never conceal it once more

.

Chapter 26
The Power of Being Seen

"Sometimes the words you write for yourself
are the ones someone else has been waiting
their whole life to read."

Creating from a place of pain can feel like writing into a void. One writes raw, unfiltered, honest words, often questioning their significance. The fear of being misunderstood or not feeling understood by others haunts the writer. For a long time, my lyrics were solely for myself. They were late-night scribbles, fragments of emotions too difficult to express aloud, pieces of my story that felt too heavy to keep inside but too loud to suppress. These lyrics served as a form of therapy, a way to survive by externalizing my pain. One day, I decided to share a piece of this with the world. It was not a song, a melody, or even a complete piece of writing. It was just words, words that came straight from the deepest part of me. When I shared these lyrics, I did not anticipate much. Part of me feared they might be overlooked or dismissed. Instead, there was unexpected silence. This silence was not the kind that felt indifferent. It was a heavy silence, as if the words struck something within them that they could not comprehend. They looked at me, almost in a whisper, and said, "Wow... I don't even know what to say." In that moment, I realized something profound: even without music, melody, or even a single note sung, my words could make an impact. They could pause someone, prompt reflection, and evoke emotions. It was not a large crowd or a grand stage. It was just one person, sitting with my lyrics and finding solace in recognizing their pain reflected in my words. That realization was enough. It proved that the story I had carried for so long was not mine. It belonged to anyone who needed to know they were not invisible in their struggles.

Reflecting on the numerous instances when I encountered lyrics in another song that deeply resonated with my emotions, I felt compelled to offer a similar moment of connection to someone else. The authenticity of my words was paramount, not in pursuit of perfection or polish, but in their ability to resonate with genuine feelings. Truth is remarkable in finding its way to those who genuinely need it. This act of sharing provided me with a profound sense of validation, affirming the weight of my words and the impact they could have on others. It revealed that even the smallest step towards expressing oneself can have a profound and far-reaching effect.

Being truly seen transcends the recognition of a significant following or viral success. It lies in the profound connection shared between individuals when they find solace and understanding in each other's words. My lyrics have touched the lives of individuals I had not spoken to in years, strangers who stumbled upon my work online, and even old friends who remained unaware of the emotional struggles I had been carrying. Their responses have been overwhelming, filled with expressions of gratitude and recognition:

"I didn't know anyone else felt this way."

"Your words gave me permission to acknowledge my own emotions."

"I've never cried from reading something before."

While fame and viral success may have allure, the true power lies in the authenticity and impact of my words. The weight of this genuine connection is far greater than any fleeting moment of attention. I have realized that my reach extends beyond the masses, directed towards those silently struggling, putting on smiles while their souls unravel. These individuals may not even be aware of the trauma they are carrying until a lyric opens the floodgates of their emotions.

The transformative power of being seen lies not in conventional notions of achieving popularity or recognition, but in the profound healing and connection it fosters. It offers solace to those in pain, assuring them of their solitude, the validity of their emotions, and the finding of understanding in shared experiences. With each message received, I embarked on a gradual healing process. Their reflections served as reminders that my pain had a purpose. My voice was not solely created for performance; it was born for connection, resonance, and breaking the silence in places that had endured it for an extended period. Previously, I held the misconception that securing a record deal was the cornerstone of embodying an artist's essence. However, I have come to a different understanding.

Becoming an artist occurs when one's authenticity liberates another. The more I shared my experiences, the more I witnessed an extraordinary transformation within myself. I shed the need to "package" my story, to tie it in a neat bow, to make it aesthetically pleasing or palatable, or to conceal the vulnerable aspects to ensure comfort for others. These vulnerable aspects embodied the essence of my power. What I previously perceived as my fragility and unworthiness were the qualities that fostered trust in others. This trust was not based on the assumption that I possessed all the answers; instead, it was because I was not pretending to have them all the time. As I became more authentic, others felt compelled to do the same. People began opening up, sharing their stories, and releasing things they had not spoken aloud in years, sometimes never. My vulnerability provided them with permission to do so. This permission was not intended for them to emulate me but to confront their own truths. The profound magic of being seen lies in the realization that when one removes the mask, they discover their true self and empower others to do the same. Rawness becomes a mirror, reflecting the essence of humanity. Suddenly, a solitary journey of survival transforms into a sacred exchange of humanity.

A single story, lyrics, or truth can profoundly impact another person. It can catalyze change, becoming the sentence, they carry when everything else crumbles, the lyric they whisper when no one else understands, or the spark that reminds them that they are not alone, that they are not crazy, and that their journey has not yet reached its conclusion. That is why I continue to write. I am no longer afraid of being exposed but of remaining hidden. I have realized that my story gains strength when shared with others, not diminishes. A profound shift within me compelled me to acknowledge a new purpose.

My creative pursuits extended beyond mere fame and a fleeting highlight reel. Instead, I sought to leave a legacy, a living, breathing testament to my existence. Each lyric I penned, each post I shared, and every moment I chose authenticity over polish contributed to this legacy. It served as a breadcrumb trail for future generations, guiding them through my journey and offering solace in knowing they were not alone. I realized that being seen was not merely about being discovered but about being witnessed. By the right individuals at the opportune moment, for the right reasons, even if it was just one person.

When someone truly saw me, encompassing my light, shadow, story, and scars, and refused to look away, that was the essence of impact. It was the purposeful visibility that subtly yet permanently transformed lives. Therefore, my writing transcended mere audibility. I sought to create space, articulate the inexpressible, lend voice to the unspoken, and provide rhythm to the silence. Perhaps, I could help others rediscover their authentic selves before the world compelled them to conceal them.

I no longer sought the spotlight; instead, I embraced the role of a beacon of light. I illuminated the path for others, one lyric, one truth, and one vulnerable moment at a time. This radical act of being seen and witnessing others, this profound connection is the true stage upon which I stand and I am already firmly planted in its embrace.

Chapter 27
One Heart at a Time
"Changing the world doesn't always start with the masses-it starts with one soul who feels less alone because of you."

*A*fter sharing my lyrics and witnessing the ensuing silence, a profound shift occurred within me. For an extended period, I harbored doubts about the significance of my words. However, I discerned the truth: my words had already resonated with someone. It was not a grand performance, a viral sensation, or a gathering of thousands applauding in unison. It was simply a single individual who paused, allowing my words to sink deeply into their soul and utter, "Wow... I resonate with that."

Inexplicably, this profound connection surpassed any standing ovation. For it illuminated the essence of this journey: it is not about fame, numbers, or seeking the limelight. It is about fostering genuine human connection. From that moment forward, I ceased preoccupying myself with the extent of my reach or the attention of those who remained unresponsive. Instead, I redirected my focus to the individuals who quietly listened, did not always respond verbally, but carried my words with them long after our conversation concluded. I realized that healing does not always transpire in grand public gatherings. It occurs one heart at a time, one person who encounters your truth and feels understood. One person carries that profound connection into their own life, and sometimes, they pass it on unknowingly, creating a ripple effect. Therefore, I continued to write, not driven by the desire to be heard by everyone but by the conviction that someone, somewhere, needed the precise words I was crafting on the page.

Even if I had never witnessed their reaction or known their name, this realization instilled a profound sense of humility. I acknowledge that my creations may never fully manifest their intended impact, yet I trust that they make a difference. It's like planting seeds in the darkness and believing they will blossom in the most unexpected locations. This journey taught me patience. The grand stage awaits, but the most profound aspect of this path lies not in the dazzling lights or the enthusiastic crowd.

In the moments preceding the release of my music, I find solitude in realizing that my words can touch one person and remind me of the profound purpose that drives me. While the prospect of achieving global recognition is appealing, I acknowledge that the impact of my music may not be confined to a massive audience. Instead, I recognize that the profound healing that can occur through my words often transpires through a single connection. Therefore, I continue to share my music with a quiet and intentional focus, trusting that the appropriate individuals will find the right words at the right time. I recognize that fulfilling my purpose lies not in achieving viral success but in making a meaningful difference in the lives of those who require it most.

I often contemplate that my music may pass by individuals who could benefit from it without ever comprehending its significance. However, I also recognize that my music was never intended for everyone, and that the individuals who truly resonate with it are the ones who do. The version of myself who once felt invisible is now being perceived through my own words, and this realization fills me with a profound sense of sanctity.

There is an undeniable beauty in the quiet individuals who rarely leave comments or express their appreciation through likes. While they may not be as vocal as others, their messages of gratitude and support hold immense value. These messages remind me that my music possesses the power to impact individuals who may not have sought it out profoundly. They testify to the transformative potential of storytelling and the enduring influence of my words.

In the past, I believed that my purpose necessitated constant attention and a level of popularity that would validate my efforts. However, I have realized that some of the most profound work occurs in silence, intimate settings, and the hearts of individuals who may never meet me. This realization brings a profound sense of peace and fulfillment, as I release myself from the need for my art to be "enough" and acknowledge its inherent value. If my words originate from my authentic truth, they will carry weight and resonate with those who require them. This is the power of storytelling, a force that transcends boundaries and weaves into the fabric of people's lives without seeking permission. When the time is right, it can heal wounds and comfort those in need. One day, someone may share with me that they read this chapter, which granted them the strength to persevere or that they printed it and affixed it to their wall. Quite possibly, they finally wrote their own story because I instilled the courage to do so. Although I may never witness all these instances, I will feel the impact in my spirit. Because the energy of this nature does not dissipate, it resonates.

If you are reading this and contemplating whether your voice matters, I want to assure you that it does. Perhaps not to the entire world simultaneously. But to someone. Somewhere. Presently and that is more than sufficient. Continue speaking. Continue appearing. Continue planting those seeds. One heart at a time is how the world transforms.

Previously, I sought signs that I was on the correct path, that my voice held significance, and that something within me was not beyond repair. However, these signs did not manifest in ostentatious displays or grand platforms. They manifested in subtle whispers. A stranger left a comment that read, "You have articulated what I could not express." I received a message at 2 a.m. that stated, "This chapter saved my life this evening." A friend approached me and said, "Do not cease. Whatever you are doing is effective." These were the signs, and they were louder than any fame could proclaim.

When you write from personal pain, your work does not merely echo your narrative. It resonates with others who are grappling with silence. If you possess the courage to remain open, even when it is uncomfortable, even when it feels as though no one is listening…You become a mirror. A lifeline. A lighthouse. It's not because you possess all the answers, but because you dared to speak when it was arduous. Being perceived this way carries a responsibility, not a burden, but a calling. I do not take it lightly. I understand the arduous search for anything that mitigates the permanence of darkness and if someone finds solace in my story, if they

186

derive strength, then my survival, every scar, every tear, every wound, was worthwhile.

Occasionally, I reflect on the chain reaction that ensues. What if my words facilitate an individual's final reconciliation with their child? What if they assist someone exiting a relationship that was diminishing their potential? What if they prevent someone from relinquishing their artistic pursuits, healing journey, or overall well-being? I may never know the truth. Nevertheless, I will continue to write as I do.

These chapters, these pages are no longer solely mine. They belong to anyone who has ever felt too quiet, shattered, or late. Anyone who has ever doubted the worth of their words. Let this serve as a reminder: You possess the capacity. If my voice can emerge from the ashes, so can yours. Together, one narrative, one heart, one courageous sentence at a time, we can effect change. A profound sanctity exists in sharing the truth before the world acknowledges your worth. It is humanities offering the gift of love before ascertaining its reception. It is faith. Not the ostentatious, polished variety that delivers speeches from elevated platforms, but the reserved, resilient variety that emerges when no applause is forthcoming. The kind that persists regardless of the outcome, driven by an unwavering conviction of one's purpose.

Each time I wield the pen now, I am no longer writing from the depths of pain. I am writing through it. With each word I write, I construct a bridge connecting my past self to my evolving self. This bridge transcends its boundaries, serving as a lifeline for those still enduring the flames of life. It reaches out to those who have yet to discover their voice, offering solace to those waiting for a sign of companionship. The extraordinary aspect lies in the realization that countless individuals are traversing life without realizing that a line I composed at the ungodly hour of 2 a.m. may one day have a profound impact on their lives. It could be a caption, a lyric, a chapter, or even a single sentence. In that moment, they will feel less isolated, not because I possessed the eloquence to craft the perfect words, but because I embodied them.

I have ceased striving to produce something that will go viral and abandoned the pursuit of captivating audiences through performance. I write as if my life depends on it, because perhaps one day, it will. The platform will expand, and the audience will gather. However, the primary objective was never to attain global recognition. It was to illuminate the world through the lens of healing. By leaving a path for others to follow, I strive to make a positive impact. If my sole purpose is alleviating someone's sense of humanity, worthiness, and understanding, then that alone is insufficient. Such an act is not merely a contribution; it is the essence of my purpose. Healing the world does not commence with public recognition; it begins with an individual who refuses to remain silent.

Chapter 28
The Ripple Effect

*"Sometimes the ones you were searching for
have been there the whole time-quietly loving
you in ways you didn't even see."*

$\mathcal{A}$s I continued to share my experiences, I observed an unexpected phenomenon. The more I spoke my truth, the more individuals who genuinely cared for me gravitated towards me. While some people distanced themselves, which is understandable, others drew closer. They did not flinch at the emotional depth of my story or shun the vulnerable aspects. Instead, they remained steadfast in their support. As the ripple of my journey spread outward, I gained a new perspective: I was not alone. I had never truly been alone. I had not consistently recognized the individuals who were truly there for me.

For an extended period, I yearned for my family, my parents and brothers, who were incapable of providing the love I required. However, I failed to recognize that my family had always been present, not by blood ties but by choice. Reflecting on my surroundings, I identified consistent individuals who never judged me or made me feel like a burden.

Mike and Tiffany, who consistently demonstrated quiet strength and care. Dalton, Mike's brother, whose presence provided a sense of calm amidst chaos. Brandon, another brother figure within

Mike's family, embodied the qualities with no comparison, not just a friend but a brother. Additionally, I recognized my lifelong anchors: Eva, who listened without judgment and reminded me of the enduring value of my heart. Lora and Zach, whose unwavering loyalty transcended distance and time. Thomas and Tommy Ray in Ohio, who assumed roles I had previously associated solely with fathers, demonstrated the essence of proper guidance and support. Jamie, who transcended the boundaries of friendship and became a sister in spirit, created a space for me without demanding anything from me. These individuals did not have to remain in my life but chose to. Their commitment is what defines them as family.

In that moment, I grasped a profound truth: family is not solely determined by blood ties. It encompasses those individuals who recognize, love, and remain steadfast through challenging times. Family is characterized by their presence, not by empty words. As I internalized this truth, a profound sense of liberation washed over me. I ceased seeking love in environments where it was unlikely to flourish. Instead, I embraced and cherished the love that had always been present in my life. This transformation was a manifestation of the ripple effect. By sharing my truth, I gained clarity in my relationships. Those who remained strengthened, while those who departed created space for more fulfilling connections. In this newfound clarity, my chosen family emerged radiant.

Furthermore, this revelation reminded me of my purpose for sharing my journey. My life is not solely about me; it extends to others. When I live my truth authentically, I permit others to do the same. It fosters compassion, broadens perspectives, and creates ripples that may not be fully comprehended.

Therefore, I continue to share my story. I do so for those who have been by my side throughout my journey, those still searching for their place in the world, and those who may not realize their chosen family awaits them.

Sometimes, the individuals who provide salvation do not bear our last names; they possess our souls. A unique form of healing emerges only after the initial grief has subsided. This healing does not occur because the pain has vanished; rather, it transpires because we finally cease to demand rationality from the pain itself. This realization resonated deeply as I grappled with the love I had been searching for within my lineage. It dawned on me that this love had been thriving in other gardens. I had been nurturing wilted roots for years, attempting to force blooms where none had ever existed. I had sought love from individuals who were adept at withholding it.

Chosen family differs. They do not compel us to remain silent in exchange for their approval. They do not offer love with a preconceived expectation of repayment. Instead, they consistently demonstrate their presence. The most unexpected revelation of this journey was that I was not merely receiving love; I was becoming someone who possessed the capacity to love fully, freely, and without apology. This transformation was shaped by the examples set by those around me, and I, in turn, adopted similar behaviors. Indeed, the profound impact of love can be likened to a ripple effect, transcending mere personal gain.

When love finds you at your most vulnerable and unworthy, it paradoxically teaches you the profound art of offering it anyway. Reflecting on my journey, I am reminded of those who remained steadfast, witnessing my rebuilding process. Their silent encouragement and unwavering support were invaluable. They applauded my efforts when no one else dared to. They offered a listening ear before my story had even gained a platform. Such love possesses a transformative power. It ceases the need for performance, self-deprecation, and the futile pursuit of worth in those who cannot appreciate it. Instead, it fosters a deep-seated belief in one's inherent worthiness, imperfections, and potential.

When individuals experience such unconditional love, they become part of a supportive network, a sanctuary, and a lasting bond. This ripple effect extends beyond mere acts of generosity and encompasses the transformative power of receiving love. Years ago, I grappled with a sense of displacement, lacking a traditional understanding of home. It was not in a house, a last name, or a bloodline that promised love but rarely delivered. Instead, I found solace on a cruise ship, seeking respite from the weight of my past.

Amidst the vibrant ambiance of the ship, Jamie entered my life. Her presence was not dramatic or ostentatious; it was simply a genuine connection, shared laughter, and the quiet realization of a haven. Our friendship transcended the ephemeral nature of time, becoming one of those rare bonds that endure. We demonstrated unwavering support for each other, qualities that were often absent in familial relationships. Years later, we eagerly anticipated another cruise, this time as chosen family, no less profound than if we had shared the same DNA.

This journey has taught me that love is not merely about giving but also about receiving. It is about embracing the transformative power of unconditional love and allowing it to shape our lives profoundly. Initially, one may question the source of their support system. However, these individuals often manifest in unexpected locations, such as encountering a stranger on a ship, discovering a family member through a close friend's connections, or receiving a heartfelt message from someone across the country who resonates deeply with you. These connections can manifest in extended conversations that transcend the boundaries of the day, or in moments of solitude, such as standing on a beach, attempting to find peace amidst emotional turmoil. They can also appear when sharing vulnerable thoughts, and instead of scrolling past, someone responds with a message expressing similar sentiment. These encounters may not always appear miraculous, but they remind us that the universe is attentive and that love can find its way when we release our rigid expectations and allow it to evolve naturally.

Reflecting on that cruise, a smile tugs at my lips, not because it was flawless, but because it marked the commencement of a profound and sacred journey. It demonstrated that healing does not always manifest in conventional ways. Sometimes, it embarks on a ship, promising solace and comfort. Sometimes, it dons a hoodie and listens more deeply than it speaks.

Occasionally, the hand extends when you remain unaware of your impending danger. Driven by this realization, I persist in writing, not seeking recognition, but rather to serve as a source of hope for those still seeking their support network. They may be found in unassuming locations, such as back porches or cruise decks, in text conversations or late-night phone calls. They are present in the tranquility that follows a panic attack and, in the silence, despite its emptiness, that exudes a profound sense of peace. These individuals are already deeply intertwined in the fabric of your life, albeit perhaps in ways you have yet to comprehend fully. Trust me, you will feel it profoundly when you finally recognize them. You will turn around and realize that the love you believed to have lost has transformed into a new and more profound form. While it may not have grown louder, it has undoubtedly become more significant. The renowned author once wisely said, "Sometimes, the individuals you were searching for have been there the entire time, quietly loving you in ways you were unaware of."

As I continued to share my words, an unexpected transformation began to unfold. As I opened my heart, I discovered that the right individuals gravitated towards me. This was not due to any desperate need for attention, but rather because the truth can attract like-minded individuals. Notably, the genuine ones drew closer when others distanced themselves. While some individuals chose to disappear, I welcomed the presence of others who deeply rooted themselves in my life. They remained steadfast and consistent, even during challenging moments. Their unwavering support was evident in their quiet presence. They consistently stood by me, offering solace and guidance. When I took the time to observe them honestly, I noticed their unwavering presence. I followed Mike and Tiffany, who were not merely friends but pillars of support. Their presence alone conveyed a profound sense of comfort and security. Their loyalty was not ostentatious, but it was sufficient to drown out the noise of those who had abandoned me. They consistently reminded me that I was never truly alone. Dalton and Brandon provided unwavering support, their presence subtly woven into the fabric of my daily life. It was as if they offered warmth and comfort, a subtle reminder that I was no longer cold. Tommy Ray and Thomas, a married couple I encountered on a cruise, left an indelible mark on my life. Their connection with me transcended mere acquaintances, as they shared wisdom, laughter, and moments of tranquility. Their unwavering love for each other and me emanated a profound sense of peace, a testament to the resilience of the human spirit. Lastly, there was Eva, a woman who embodied the essence of a mother. Her love was not grand or ostentatious but relatively quiet protection and a gentle presence. Her ability to sense when to check in, listen, and uplift my spirits without uttering a word demonstrated that sometimes, the mothers we need are not those we are born to but those who are divinely appointed to guide us. Lora and Brett's high school memories have become lifelong anchors. Their love was never performative; it was genuine and enduring. Their children, affectionately calling me Uncle Mark, profoundly impacted me. Being accepted and loved unconditionally by those I cherish deeply fills my void. Despite not sharing blood ties, I cannot overlook Dakota, my sister in spirit. She possessed an uncanny ability to discern through facades and silence, standing by my side without seeking a filtered version of myself. She demonstrated that true sisterhood transcends formal permission and exists.

These individuals did not appear randomly; they were sent to me. They were the answers to my prayers during moments of vulnerability and despair. They provided the safety I sought when I was breaking. They served as proof that even when my birth family failed me, my chosen family can find me and love me more profoundly. I believed that "family" was an inherent right, something one was automatically born into. However, I have realized that DNA does not define family. It is characterized by devotion. Family is defined by those who remain steadfast even in the face of adversity. They never waver, even when holding onto intricate narratives becomes burdensome. These individuals have been my unwavering support system, lifting me when needed. They have consistently reminded me of my inherent worthiness of love throughout my life's journey.

I may not bear their surnames, I possess something more profound, their unwavering loyalty, infectious laughter, and unconditional love. These qualities embody the very essence of a genuine family

.

Chapter 29
The Strength in Letting Go
"Letting go doesn't mean you stop caring. It means you stop carrying what was never yours to hold."

I persistently endeavored to maintain my grip on hope for an extended period. I yearned for my parents to reciprocate my love, my brothers to stand in solidarity with me, and even a fractured family to reconcile. However, it proved futile each time I reached out to this hope. It was akin to attempting to grasp shattered glass. This realization was reminiscent of the night my husband abruptly shattered our marriage certificate upon the floor. I vividly recall the sound, the sharp, violent crack of the frame striking the ground, and the glass fragmenting into scattered pieces. In that moment, I stood barefoot, momentarily immobilized, before instinctively bending down to attempt cleaning up the mess. Unbeknownst to me, this act resulted in a self-inflicted injury as I sliced my feet open. I experienced bleeding as I desperately endeavored to collect the shards, yearning to hold onto something that was irreparably damaged. This experience mirrored my emotional state with my family. I was bleeding for something that could never be restored. I was attempting to hold onto individuals who were incapable of providing the love I consistently sought. Every futile attempt, I inflicted further self-harm. Conceiving that the individuals we desire most will never fulfill our needs causes a peculiar form of grief.

This grief is not audible; it is a quiet ache that permeates our bones upon the realization that, regardless of our love for them, they cannot reciprocate it as our souls require. I engaged in various attempts to rectify the situation. I endeavored to demonstrate my worthiness, maintained silence, and retreated into a smaller persona. I amplified my voice, but none of these actions yielded any positive outcome. As my efforts intensified, the pain intensified exponentially. A profound realization struck me: I was not losing them; they had already departed. I was truly losing the illusion that they would ever fulfill my expectations. Letting go did not occur in a dramatic, monumental moment. The biggest hearts of them all, sometimes require decades to heal and step into their fullest potential. It unfolds gradually, comprising numerous instances of self-awareness that compelled me to cease sacrificing for individuals who remained oblivious to my struggles. The decision to stop answering calls only served to reopen emotional wounds. The decision was made to cease replaying the past in the hope of altering its outcome. It was acknowledging my love for them while recognizing the strain it was causing me. Allowing go did not imply a cessation of care. I still wish them peace and hope they will find healing. However, I finally comprehended that my peace could not be contingent upon their choices. Forgiveness came not for their sake but for mine. Forgiveness is not about excusing their actions but about releasing the emotional burden they had on me. It is about asserting that I refuse to let this pain define the remainder of my life. In this release, I experienced a sense of liberation. It was not due to the disappearance of memories but because I no longer allowed them to control me.

I surveyed my life, observing the individuals who truly demonstrated their presence, my chosen family, my steadfast friends, and those who reminded me of the essence of genuine love. I realized a profound truth: I was not devoid of substance; I was brimming with the right people, possibilities, and a future that did not require the validation of the past. By releasing myself from the burdens never meant for me, I created space for healing, music, and the purpose that awaited me. This decision was not a sign of weakness, but rather a manifestation of strength, the strength that requires the courage to assert: "I love you… But I love myself more." Therefore, I released myself, not with anger or hatred, but with peace that finally liberated me after all these years. Following my release, I anticipated grief and guilt, but what I did not expect was stillness.

A peculiar, almost sacred silence descended upon my life, the kind that only descends after the storm, leaving behind the remnants of the past and the choice to rebuild. Initially, I was uncertain of how to navigate this newfound tranquility. For many years, I had been enveloped in noise. Internal conflicts, imagined conversations, and cycles of shame and longing plagued me. However, the silence that once felt empty now held a sacred quality, serving as a pristine canvas for new beginnings. For the first time in my life, I was liberated from the constraints of external approval, free to express myself without inhibition and to be seen for my authentic self, not merely for my survival. The release of those who held me captive did not leave a void; instead, it cleared the path for personal growth and empowerment. Standing in the center of this newfound freedom, I no longer awaited external validation or sought recognition for my worth.

Instead, I embraced my wholeness and worthiness, recognizing that I had been chosen by a force far greater than myself. The absence of their voices paved the way for a profound transformation. I found solace in the guidance of my soul and the whisper of purpose that had long eluded me amidst the chaos.

Once again, writing, singing, and creating became avenues for expression, fueled by a newfound strength derived from the absence of pain and the embrace of power. I discovered that the peace I sought was not fragile or transient but deeply rooted and unshakable. It emanated from within, a testament to my self-acceptance and self-love. While healing is not a linear journey, I acknowledge that there are moments when I miss them or replay past moments, questioning my decisions. However, most days, I find solace in deep breathing, laughter, and a renewed sense of freedom.

The strength gained from letting go extends beyond mere release; it encompasses reclamation. It reclaims my time, energy, voice, and worth, liberating me from walking on eggshells and waiting for unfulfilled expectations. A profound joy fills my life, a subtle yet authentic sensation akin to waking up to sunlight after a prolonged period of rain, hearing my voice and realizing its inherent beauty, or catching my reflection without flinching but smiling. This transformative journey has granted me the freedom to breathe, evolve, and rise above the limitations of the past. Henceforth, I shall never again apologize for prioritizing peace over performance. I shall never again plead for love that demands my silence. I shall never again bear the weight of what was never mine to hold. I have finally grasped the profound truth: Letting go was not the culmination of my existence.

It was the genesis of something far more transformative.

As the days passed, I gradually understood the extent of my life spent in anticipation. I had been waiting for invitations, validation, and love in the language of my heart, yet it remained unspoken. However, letting go transcended the release of others. It liberated me from the shackles of seeking permission. I no longer required their acknowledgment of my pain for it to be authentic. I no longer sought an apology as a prerequisite for healing. And I certainly did not need a family reunion to validate my sense of belonging, for I had already discovered that sanctuary within myself. I ceased attempting to maintain relationships that hindered my growth. I stopped editing my authentic self to accommodate others' comfort. I ceased replaying moments of regret, acknowledging that the silence had already spoken volumes. In that liberated space, a profound transformation unfolded. Wholeness emerged; not the superficial kind that seeks external validation, but the authentic, earned kind that demands effort and resilience. The kind that arises from adversity, where the decision to rebuild emerges even without external recognition. I embraced the version of myself who no longer harbored constant expectations of disappointment. I stood tall in any room, unwavering in my presence. I refrained from second-guessing my words or over-explaining my truths. This version of myself was not born from applause; it emerged from the ashes of the past, nurtured by the quiet determination to rise, even when no one was watching.

Letting go unlocked the keys to a kingdom I had never known existed. It granted me freedom, peace, a voice, and a purpose. I embarked on a journey of rebuilding, not with the remnants of the past, but with the fire that had always simmered beneath its surface. Individuals began to notice my change as I embarked on this transformative journey. Their attention was not a result of my seeking validation, but a natural consequence of my growth and authenticity. When one embraces their authentic self, a profound transformation occurs. Individuals shift their perspectives, soften their boundaries, and inspire others to speak the truth. True strength lies in letting go of expectations and taking decisive action. It involves ceasing to seek validation and instead walking confidently in one's path. This liberation allows individuals to stop bleeding for love's sake and avoid situations that only bring pain. It enables them to rest, rise, and find fulfillment, even if their efforts are not met with immediate recognition. The version of myself who sought validation through superficial means has vanished, replaced by a man who nurtures his sense of belonging by surrounding himself with those who uplift him. Letting go has not only set me free; it has reclaimed my true self. There is a sacredness in the moment when one ceases to seek belonging and embraces silence after relentlessly pursuing what is fleeting. This silence is not empty; it is filled with the echoes of one's breath, heartbeat, and finally, their voice, resonating after years of being drowned out by the expectations of others. I did not merely abandon people; I returned to myself. I reclaimed the child who yearned to be seen, the teenager who held back tears in the darkness, and the man who offered unwavering loyalty in environments that could not sustain it. I approached them with reverence, acknowledging their resilience in overcoming the attempts to silence them. I owe them an immense debt of gratitude. Letting go taught me that healing does not entail forgetting. It involves honoring the chapters of one's life without allowing them to define the outcome.

These lessons remain deeply ingrained in my memory, and the pain I endured still lingers. However, my perspective has shifted, and I now walk with a newfound purpose. I no longer perceive myself as discarded; instead, I recognize the gold within the rubble of my past. Remarkably, when I ceased looking back, life opened before me, presenting new opportunities and possibilities. Doors that I did not even knock on began creaking open. Individuals with whom I never anticipated encountering became family in spirit. Opportunities, clarity, and peace surged when I made space for them. That is the essence of release. Initially, it may feel akin to loss. However, it is preparation.

I do not define love solely by the duration of someone's presence. Instead, I define it by the individual who stood closest to me when I was most vulnerable and did not falter. Individuals like Mike and Tiffany did not merely appear during holidays or for convenience. They arrived silently during storms, and sacred moments transcended the need for verbal communication. They became anchors when I was unknowingly drifting. Individuals such as Tommy Ray and Thomas, with whom I encountered on a cruise, yet I felt as though I had known them for an eternity. They enveloped me in laughter, wisdom, and a comforting embrace that instilled in me the belief that there was a place for someone like me. They were the family I had not recognized I was missing. Not by blood. But by a profound connection.

Upon examining my life now, with its imperfections and setbacks, I have discovered something unexpected: Wholeness. Not perfection, but wholeness, constructed upon the foundation of truth, brick by brick. Breath by breath.

If you are holding onto something causing you more harm than benefit, this serves as a clear indication. You are permitted to release it. Don't think that you're surrendering, more so that you are finally returning home to yourself. I assure you: That is where the strength has been concealed all along

Chapter 30
Walking Into Freedom

"Freedom isn't always a loud celebration.
Sometimes it's the relief of no longer carrying
what was breaking you."

*A*fter releasing the weight of my burdens, a profound stillness descended upon me. For an extended period, my life had been characterized by a ceaseless noise, a relentless pursuit of self-validation, the replay of past conversations, and the gnawing guilt and shame associated with contemplating escape. However, once I liberated myself from these constraints, the ensuing silence was initially disorienting, like emerging from a crowded room into the vast expanse of open air. It was only after realizing the immense burden I had carried that I could finally breathe.

The path to freedom did not manifest in grand fireworks or a public declaration. Instead, it felt like awakening from a state of perpetual heaviness, as if the weight on my chest had vanished. It was no longer a matter of flinching at the sound of my phone buzzing, fearing another message that would inflict pain. Instead, I found myself liberated from the need to defend myself.

For the first time, I experienced a sense of lightness, a clarity that allowed me to think, dream without unease, and embark on a journey towards the future rather than being ensnared by the past. I began to perceive the world with renewed eyesight in this newfound freedom. I noticed the small joys that had eluded me during my struggles, the kindness of those who remained steadfast in their support, and the beauty that lay in the quiet moments I had once hurried through. Freedom granted me the space to rediscover the essence of life. Bestowed upon me was a sense of clarity. When one is no longer burdened by those who do not love them, it becomes possible to discern the true nature of those who do. One can finally hear their voice, unhindered by external distractions and finally, one can chart a course towards one's true destiny. I came to realize that freedom is not merely the absence of pain. It is the presence of possibility, the realization that one's past does not dictate the outcome of one's life. It is the power to shape one's narrative. This journey was not about escaping from reality. It was about making a conscious choice that prioritized peace over chaos, healing over cycles, and self-discovery over self-destruction. It was about embracing my fullness, flaws, and all. Embracing freedom felt like standing on the edge of an uncharted territory. I was uncertain of the challenges that awaited me, but I was confident that I would surpass the limitations imposed upon me by my past. For anything constructed upon truth, self-love, and peace invariably surpasses the constructs built upon pain. For the first time in an extended period, I was no longer consumed by apprehension regarding the future.

The silence did not merely bring tranquility; it catalyzed a reckoning. When the clamor ceased, I could finally discern the underlying truths beneath the surface, and what I perceived was my authentic self. My voice initially timid, as if it had not been used in years was finally mine. It was unburdened by shame or obligation. Let alone it did not conform to the expectations of those who had never truly comprehended me. It was raw, honest, and liberated. Freedom did not imply that I possessed all the answers. However, it liberated me from the self-deception that had hindered my growth. I no longer felt compelled to feign well-being solely to maintain harmony. I no longer felt obligated to diminish my truth to accommodate the comfort of others nor did I feel compelled to apologize for existing in a manner that unsettled them.

In a gradual process of self-discovery and transformation, I implemented subtle changes in my behavior. I declined requests without harboring guilt, prioritizing my desires over those of others, and confronting my emotions rather than suppressing them. Slowly, life responded to these transformative shifts. New opportunities emerged, not through forceful manipulation, but because I had finally aligned myself with the authentic version of myself destined to navigate those opportunities. Admittedly, there were moments of solitude and loneliness, as letting go entails relinquishing familiar entities, even if they were detrimental to my well-being. However, in those hushed moments, I discovered a profound sense of belonging; a connection that transcended the confines of individuals or groups. I no longer sought love that should have been freely bestowed upon me. I no longer tolerated confusion and mistook it for hope. I no longer romanticized individuals who could only offer fragmented expressions of love. I had achieved wholeness and no longer sought validation from others.

The true essence of freedom does not merely alter external circumstances; it transforms the nature of one's being. This transformation profoundly alters one's perception of oneself. One moves with a newfound grace, exuding a sense of deservingness. Speaking becomes more assertive, free from the constraints of fear. Building projects are undertaken without seeking permission, driven by a sense of self-reliance. This shift catalyzes a profound transformation. It does not stem from external pursuit but from embracing one's true self. Peace, clarity, direction, and love emerge not only from external sources but also from within. This newfound freedom liberates individuals from the layers of self-imposed limitations.

The masks worn to maintain harmony, the roles adopted to feel worthy, and the silence maintained to conform to societal expectations are shed. This process unfolds gradually and reverently, akin to the natural shedding of old skin or the realization of a body that finally feels like home.

Ceasing to perform, over-explain, and presenting rehearsed versions of one's truth to ensure the comfort of others paved the way for personal growth. Instead, the focus shifted towards becoming the authentic self, free from the trauma, guilt, and manipulative love that had previously defined them.

Singing once again became a means of healing, not seeking applause, but as a form of self-expression. Writing served as a means of remembering one's identity, not as a means of impressing others. Entering rooms no longer involved questioning whether one was too much, but rather contemplating whether the space could accommodate the fullness of someone who had finally discovered their worth.

Freedom transcended a fleeting moment; it represented a return to a younger, dreamer version of oneself before the world taught them to dim their light. It was a return to the man who emerged from the ashes, affirming, "There is still more for me." It was a return to the truth that one had never been broken but instead buried.

Currently, I rise with gratitude for those who remained by my side, the wisdom gained through tough times, and the voice that was once silenced, now resonates with power. There is an inherent beauty in walking in freedom with quiet grace, no need to proclaim it or prove its existence. Embrace the journey of self-discovery and liberation. Those destined to accompany you on this path will discern your authentic stride and feel your presence. Freedom has a distinct frequency, attracting the right individuals when embodied. As the song "Freedom Is the Homecoming" suggests, the journey is not about becoming someone else but about returning to the essence of oneself that was never afraid. Freedom has profoundly transformed my perception of the world. I believed freedom entailed escaping from pain, relationships, and the past. However, I have gained a deeper understanding: true freedom does not involve running away; it consists of returning home. Home to the heart that still pulses with hope despite adversity. Home to the voice that once whispered softly but now speaks with conviction.

I found solace and fulfillment in the realm of my purpose, which I always believed I had to earn. I do not owe anyone an explanation for my transformation, nor do I need to reopen old wounds to demonstrate my healing. My peace is unwavering, my joy is genuine, and my growth is unrequited permission, it simply exists. Along the way, I ceased striving to make others comfortable with my healing. Conforming to the past would dishonor the miracle of my present self. I have shed blood for this freedom, wept for it, and fought battles unseen, emerging with scars that now gleam like armor. Freedom has taught me that I do not need to carry broken glass to prove my past hurts. I do not need to justify my boundaries by explaining my pain, and I do not need to return to a place simply because someone finally acknowledges my absence. This life, the one I am currently living, is mine. It is not built on fear, approval, or shame. Instead, it is rooted in truth, illuminated by divine timing, and fueled by the elements that once threatened to destroy me. As a result, I awoke with a newfound perspective. I open my eyes without anticipating pain.

As I step outside, I bask in the sunlight, feeling its warmth. I recognize that the sun's rays are not just for me; they are a testament to the abundance of life and creativity surrounding me. I engage in acts of creation, expression, and love, not driven by necessity, but by an overflowing sense of purpose.

When you finally attain freedom, you cease to seek a place at tables that were never designed to accommodate your brilliance. Instead, you construct your own, a sanctuary where you can express yourself authentically. You invite peace to join you in this sanctuary, cherishing it daily. This is the true triumph: not merely surviving the challenges that attempt to diminish you but transforming yourself into a complete and more empowered individual. As you walk forward with clarity in your vision, a sense of strength in your shoulders, and an openness in your heart, you realize that you have transcended the limitations of the past and embraced the boundless possibilities of freedom.

Chapter 31
The Next Chapter Begins
"Every ending is just the beginning of something truer."

A profound sense of clarity emerges, accompanied by a renewed sense of purpose. My life no longer appears solely as a collection of distressing memories but as an ongoing narrative with the potential for profound meaning beyond suffering. For an extended period, I erroneously believed that pain was the sole purpose of my existence. However, I now comprehend that pain serves as the fertile ground, nurturing the seeds of genuine purpose. My voice, words, and music have manifested as the embodiment of this purpose. All those nights spent crafting lyrics that may never be read, all those quiet moments spent playing melodies on my guitar, even when unheard, and all the times I share my story and witness its profound impact on others—these moments have led me to this pivotal juncture.

This forthcoming chapter in my life transcends mere healing; it encompasses the role of becoming a conduit for others. I recognize that every challenge I have overcome, every moment I believed would shatter me, has prepared me to reach those still trapped in their darkness. Music has transcended its role as mere entertainment; it has become a bridge, a means of expressing the inexpressible and reaching the depths of another's soul. It serves as a reminder that beauty and hope persist even in the darkest corners. Although I may not yet be gracing the grand stage, I am diligently constructing it as we speak. I am laying the foundation for my future success with every lyric I pen, every melody I compose, and every moment I choose to embrace healing rather than concealment.

Although the spotlight may not yet be present, the preparations are well underway. I am confident that when the time is right, the stage will be ready, as I will be fully prepared. This chapter is not about hastening progress; it is about aligning my heart with my purpose, my energy with the future I aspire to, and my story with the divine calling that has been patiently awaiting me. I no longer perceive my past as a burden to be concealed; instead, I view it as a valuable chapter in my journey, a testament to my resilience and growth. I perceive it as a catalyst for growth and transformation. It serves as fuel for my musical expression, my healing journey, and my profound connection with the world.

For the first time, I no longer merely aspire to become a global voice; I firmly believe in my potential. The pursuit of fame does not drive this belief; rather, it is the realization that my journey transcends personal boundaries. This chapter of my life is not about forgetting my roots; rather, it is about honoring them by transforming them into a source of hope for others.

As I survey my life, the freedom I have fought for, the unwavering support of my chosen family, the words I have penned, and the melodies still forming within me, I am filled with a sense of purpose. I recognize that this is the commencement of a significant chapter in my life, the authentic beginning. The pain that once shaped my narrative has not been a destructive force but has sculpted me into a deeper, broader individual. It has created a space within me that is vast enough to accommodate the unique voice that the world has yet to hear. In truth, I do not believe that my purpose has been solely to heal and move on. My purpose has been to rise with a resounding voice that resonates with the world. The nights spent in my car, replaying painful memories and questioning my place in this world, were not wasted. They were invaluable rehearsals, training grounds, and moments of self-discovery that prepared me for my destined role.

These moments allowed me to empathize with others' silent suffering, enabling me to offer them solace and understanding. I understand that being chosen is not about achieving perfection but being willing to endure challenges and emerge stronger. It is about using one's scars as guiding principles, sharing one's story with vulnerability and acceptance, even when imperfect, misunderstood, or uncomfortable. This upcoming chapter of my life is not about seeking validation or recognition from others. It is about embracing my journey, fulfilling my purpose, and positively impacting the world. Presence, alignment, and authenticity are the cornerstones of this journey. I commit to showing up thoroughly daily, even if my efforts remain unnoticed. This unwavering commitment is the catalyst for growth. When I authentically express myself, unburdened by masks, filters, or apologies, I resonate with others. My voice transcends mere echoes and lands with impact.

Deep within my core, I experience an overwhelming sense of fulfillment. I am transcending the constraints of a new season and embracing my authentic self. This transformative process marks the cessation of echoes and the commencement of an anthem. I am not merely writing my story but composing it, one lyric, truth, and heart at a time.

Retrospectively, I recognize the extent of my self-doubt and the numerous instances where I sought validation from the wrong individuals. I attempted to conform to spaces not meant for me, diminishing my authentic self. However, I have evolved into a new version of myself. Imperfections no longer define my journey; they are guided by rediscovering my identity. I was never broken; I was being rebuilt and restructured for a purpose greater than my imagination. Each setback served as a blueprint for this exact version of the one who no longer flinches at silence, seeks understanding through silence, and prioritizes peace over proximity. There is a sacredness in this journey phase, where I no longer seek a seat at the table; instead, I am constructing my legacy.

This transformation is not born of bitterness but of vision, divine trust, and an unwavering conviction proclaiming, "I was built for this. Each lyric I compose carries the weight of generations of silence being shattered. Every time I press record, I am not merely singing but testifying. Every post I share, every performance I prepare for, every dream I dare to speak aloud is not random; a higher purpose guides it. This journey transcends algorithms and applause; it aligns with the legacy I aspire to create. I am no longer confined to the next chapter but embarking on an eternal odyssey of self-discovery and growth. This is the mission: This is the divine assignment: Not merely to heal, but to activate. To remind individuals of their inherent worth when the world has forgotten it. To express what others are too timid to utter. To compose what generations were taught to suppress. I used to question, "Why me?" Now, I pose, "Why not me?" After enduring all I have survived, every time I contemplated succumbing, I refrained. After every scar that transformed into a song, how could I doubt my selection?

This forthcoming chapter is not a mere comeback; it is a coronation. For the version of myself emerging is not pursuing a dream; rather, it is embodying it. Previously, I perceived the dream as an elusive entity that required pursuit, capture, or persuasion from the world to acknowledge my deservingness. However, my perspective has evolved. The dream has continuously resided within me; the crown has always been mine. I merely needed to cease bestowing it upon individuals incapable of perceiving it.

This chapter is not about arrival; it is about remembrance. It is about recalling the child who hummed melodies to sustain themselves. It is about remembering the adolescent who secretly scribbled lyrics, hoping someone would notice. It is about the man repeatedly brought to his knees but persisted in rising with a pen and a resolute spirit. I am not here to impress anyone; instead, I am here to make a profound impact. I am here to create moments that rekindle the essence of life in individuals. I am here to provide language to the wounds that remain ineffable. I am here to sing for those who have been silenced and embody my essence from when I was younger.

The world finally turns its attention and inquires, "Where did he originate from?" The response will be straightforward: I did not emerge from obscurity. I emerged from pain, prayer, perseverance, and purpose. I originated from the darkness, yet I never truly belonged to it. I carried light throughout my journey, finally unleashing its radiance. Therefore, let this chapter serve as the anthem of a man reborn. A man who ceased awaiting permission. A man who ceased nurturing lifeless endeavors. A man who recognized that his voice is not merely a gift but a weapon. A healer, a portal, and a legacy. Previously, I wrote solely for survival. Now, I am writing for awakening and the next time you encounter me, I will be on that stage not merely as a performer, but as a conduit. For the boy who once whispered into the darkness…Is now singing to the world.

Chapter 32
Becoming the Messenger

"Your story isn't just yours-it's a lifeline for someone else who thinks they're drowning alone."

$\mathscr{A}$t a pivotal juncture, I realized that my pain was not an isolated incident but a consequence of my actions, empowering me to transform it into a message that resonates with others. For an extended period, I dedicated myself solely to writing and reflecting as a means of survival. My words served as a therapeutic outlet, and my lyrics provided a channel for expressing my authentic truth. However, I now perceive my work beyond personal catharsis. Each lyric I compose and each story I share transcends my own experiences. They serve as a beacon of hope for individuals who have yet to discover their voice, those burdened by the weight of their struggles, and those who feel isolated in their pain.

This realization has transformed me from an aspiring artist into a messenger. Music has always transcended mere sound for me; it is a language for the inexpressible, a means of transforming overwhelming emotions into healing balm. My narrative, once a source of self-loathing, has become the very essence of my voice. People connect with authenticity, not with perfection. I envision myself as a beacon of support for those who have experienced my struggles, offering them solace and reassurance through my music.

This calling transcends the allure of fame and the spotlight. It is a profound sense of service, dedicated to those who remain in the shadows of silence, shame, and despair, questioning the inherent meaning of their lives beyond their pain. Embracing the role of a messenger demands courage and vulnerability. It entails allowing my scars to speak, not as open wounds, but as tangible evidence of the transformative power of healing. While I may not possess all the answers, I am committed to the journey of learning and growth. I recognize this truth: If my voice can inspire someone to persevere, if my words can illuminate even one person's darkness, then every experience I have endured will have been worthwhile.

Previously, I believed my purpose was to discover my true self. However, I now comprehend that my purpose is to give myself away, not in fragmented pieces or amidst pain, but in authenticity, art, music, and connection. This is what it means to become a messenger. I want to transform what attempted to destroy me into a message that uplifts and supports another individual. To live in a manner that conveys:

"If I can overcome challenges, you can as well."

I am not merely surviving my narrative but carrying it forward and I am prepared to deliver it to those who require it most. Realizing that my story is no longer solely for my consumption creates a profound sense of sanctity. It is akin to carrying a torch. You recall the fire that ignited it, the burns it inflicted upon your hands... but now you elevate it high, not to display the scars, but to illuminate the path for another. This is the posture I am learning to adopt now. Not as a victim, nor merely as a survivor. But as a conduit. A channel. A reminder.

What I have endured, every betrayal, silent cry, and fragment of heartbreak has not merely shaped me; it has positioned me. It has aligned me with the individuals who need to comprehend that resilience possesses a melody. And that melody resonates with truth. It resonates with vulnerability. It resonates with someone who has traversed the flames and emerged with a song rather than bitterness.

Previously, I held the misconception that my voice would only be heard by a million individuals. However, I now comprehend that if I impart hope into the heart of just one soul, that echo will transcend the boundaries of my knowledge. This is the modus operandi of messengers. They do not seek fame; they possess an unwavering intention. They do not generate noise; they impart impact. As the adage goes, the most profound messages are not uttered aloud; they are felt and this is the aspiration I hold for my music. Not merely catchy lyrics, but lifelines. Soft landing points for arduous narratives. Safe environments for fragmented pieces to disintegrate and be reassembled with elegance.

Thus, I write. Therefore, I share. Thus, I sing even if the room is empty or the platform is diminutive. Even if no one applauds, for the individual who requires it most, it may be listening in silence and if they discern what I never had the opportunity to hear, "You remain deserving," "You continue to hold significance," "You are not beyond redemption", then I have fulfilled my purpose. This is the message. This is my mission. And I am merely commencing. A hushed transformation occurs when one's anguish transforms into a purposeful endeavor.

One ceases to feel compelled to elucidate one's journey to everyone. One ceases to harbor the hope that individuals will comprehend the depths of their experiences. For deep within, one finally comprehends that one was never destined to be understood by everyone. One was destined to be received by the appropriate individuals. These are the individuals I address now. These are the individuals who comprehend the experience of weeping in silence. These are the individuals who suppress their screams. These individuals question their worth because someone else failed to perceive it.

As a former resident of these places, I know their significance. Now that I have emerged from the darkness, I am responsible for extending an invitation to the following individual attempting to depart from that same abyss.

This chapter of my life does not require approval or applause. It demands truth, spoken, sung, or shared; even if it unsettles me or reveals my most vulnerable and unhealed aspects. The world does not demand perfection; it demands authenticity. It requires narratives like mine proclaiming, "You can endure what you believed would annihilate you."

Narratives that assert, "There exists life beyond the numbness." Narratives that proclaim, "Your voice is not too late. You are precisely on time."

When I finally embraced my role as the messenger, I ceased to diminish or play it small. This is not about ego; it is about an assignment. They do not await their full readiness when called to be a messenger. They speak, nonetheless. They sing, nonetheless. With a trembling voice and a heart full of truth, I trust that my vulnerability is sufficient. I feel a sense of wholeness growing whenever I share my authentic self. Every time I pour out my truth, I am filled with a sense of fulfillment. This paradoxical nature of being a messenger is a constant reminder that giving is the key to receiving.

Whether my music achieves mainstream success or not, if it touches the life of one soul with the power of healing, I have fulfilled my purpose. I was never driven by numbers or fame but by the profound meaning that music holds for me. Now that I have discovered this meaning, I am determined to hold on to it.

In the past, I believed that my message required refinement, that I needed greater sophistication, and that I had to wait until my past experiences had healed and my narrative had reached perfection. However, I have realized that the most impactful messengers are those who speak while they are still in the throes of healing, share their experiences while their voices tremble, and possess the courage to be candid.

I no longer harbor shame regarding my past experiences, for each valley I have traversed has shaped the path I guide others on. Each night, I grappled with self-doubt, questioning my worthiness and wondering if I made a difference and if I was preparing for the day, I would assist someone else in answering the same existential query.

This calling on my life is not a performance but a responsibility. It is deeply ingrained in my soul, forged in adversity, and held with reverence. I comprehend the struggle of nearly succumbing to despair, the fear of becoming invisible even in a crowded room, and the anguish of drowning in a sea of uncertainty.

If I can serve as a voice that shatters that silence for another, if I can be the melody that prompts someone to pause and feel seen, then I will persist, even if the audience is small, the doors are slow to open, or it takes years for the world to recognize my efforts.

Writing, singing, and speaking are not effortless endeavors but indispensable. They are essential for me and for those who continue to grapple with struggle. They are crucial for those who are drowning in fear and uncertainty.

Some individuals persist in questioning their autonomy. I aspire to fulfill that question by living a life that embodies hope and inspiration. My music aims to provide solace in the silence of others. Assuming the role of messenger transcends a mere title, constituting a solemn commitment. My unwavering vow is to diligently seek the light I have sought and gently place it in the hands of another.

Chapter 33
Preparing the Offering

"Before you give your gift to the world, it must first be nurtured, shaped, and honored within you."

$\mathcal{U}$pon comprehending my role as a messenger rather than solely an artist, my approach to music and words underwent a transformative shift. Once mere fragments of my healing journey, my lyrics evolved into offerings to be shared with others.

I delved into the notebooks and phone saved with my lyrics, encountering raw and unfinished pieces and scattered thoughts from late nights seeking emotional release. However, upon revisiting these writings, I discerned beyond pain, messages of resilience, survival, and solace. These messages could remind someone else, "You are still present, and your existence matters." With this newfound purpose, I embarked on a refining process, not driven by perfectionism, but by the desire for clarity. Each note became an intentional expression of emotion, crafted to evoke a profound connection with listeners. It was as if I was gathering every experience, every scar, every tear, and every moment of doubt, transforming them into a beautiful tapestry that transcended my identity.

Preparing this offering was not a hurried endeavor but a deliberate and sacred process. Time, patience, and reverence are essential when offering a piece of one's soul.

This period also brought discipline, not in a harsh sense, but in the loving form, emphasizing self-honor and respect. I continued to write, practice, revisit past lessons, and anticipate the future.

Urgency was absent, for I recognized that preparation was integral to the purpose. As seeds require time to bloom, so does an artist's calling. The quiet, unseen work I engaged in was as crucial as the day my music would finally resonate with the world. As I prepared, I could almost envision the day I would stand before an audience, the day the lights would illuminate, and the music would commence. When that moment arrived, it would transcend mere performance and become an offering, a profound connection, a healing balm, and an exposition of truth.

I am not rushing this endeavor; instead, I am meticulously constructing it, piece by piece, word by word, note by note. When I finally present this gift to the world, I aspire for it all to carry the weight, healing, and love it was intended to convey.

This is not merely music; it is my narrative, transformed. It is my anguish, redeemed. It is my purpose, unfolding. Soon, it will no longer be confined to my possession. A sacredness exists in the interim, the seasons when no one is present to witness. When the applause has not yet arrived, and you persistently dedicate yourself to the page, the practice, and the promise, simply because you believe; that is where I resided. I refrained from pursuing perfection and seeking approval through performance. Instead, I immersed myself in the arduous preparation process, allowing it to purge what was essential and discard what was not.

Occasionally, I would find safe haven in the quietude of my room, accompanied only by my guitar. At other times, I would hum melodies in the privacy of my car, testing their resonance in the mundane aspects of everyday life. These were no longer mere songs; they had become fragments of my essence refined, reimagined, and shaped by every tear, every prayer, and every breakthrough. I was not merely composing a setlist but preparing a sacrifice, a testament to truth and testimony.

There were moments when I grappled with the uncertainty of whether I would ever attain readiness. I questioned whether the world would comprehend the essence of my message. I doubted the adequacy of my sound and my worthiness. However, each time these doubts assailed me, I found solace in a deeper, more profound source than fear.

Intention: I reminded myself that this offering was not intended for approval but for alignment. The intended recipients would perceive its authenticity because it emanated from a source beyond mere performance. There is a rationale behind the sacredness of specific endeavors, including the disappearance and subsequent reappearance of prophets and poets and the delayed blooming of trees after enduring winter. I was not concealing myself but rather in a state of formation, allowing each note to attain greater precision and each lyric to acquire greater weight. I permitted the message to percolate within my being until it transcended the painful perception and embraced the essence of freedom.

It is essential to recognize that preparation is the essence of the offering. The creations we nurture in the shadows are the very essence that resonates with others in the light. When the moment arrives, when the music finally encounters the microphone, the world will not merely perceive sound; they will experience substance because the creation was not rushed, filtered, or manufactured. It emerged from the depths of silence, the essence of the spirit, and the transformative power of fire.

When the time comes to share this offering, I will not be performing; instead, I will be reflecting. I will recall my journey, my initial aspirations, and the reasons that sustained me. I will remember those who did not make it and who required these songs as sustenance. This offering, this music, and this message were never crafted for entertainment purposes but for awakening. Not long ago, I gazed upon my writings and questioned my significance. However, I was reminded that I was not writing to impress but to survive. There were nights when I doubted my ability to endure, but I embraced my vulnerability instead of succumbing. These lyrics and stories were never about fame or validation; they served as a beacon of guidance, a map for those who might find themselves lost in the same darkness.

Previously, I held the misconception that art required meticulous refinement, perfection, and marketability. However, I have realized that authentic art emerges from vulnerability and imperfection. Words may flow with unruly force, and melodies may tremble under the weight of emotion. These imperfections are where true value lies, not in striving for perfection, but in embracing the presence of the artist's soul. My offering would not be sterile or devoid of honesty. It would provide permission for individuals to feel, to grieve, to release, and to embark on new beginnings.

Holding the microphone carries profound responsibility. It extends beyond mere words; it encompasses the energy, healing, and truth conveyed through music. I aspire to create music that transcends the boundaries of a song, becoming a mirror that reflects the essence of the soul and whispers, "You are still here, and your presence matters."

In preparation for this sacred offering, I dedicated myself to music and my growth and well-being. I became mindful of the impact of my choices, the people I surrounded myself with, the energy I allowed into my space and honored my voice with reverence, recognizing its significance not only for myself but also for the potential impact it may have on others.

My prayer, practice, and speech transformed, guided by reverence rather than ego. I understood that this offering was for me and those who may find solace or inspiration in my music. It reached out to the silent crier at 2 a.m., the teenager who doubted their voice, and the adult still carrying the wounds of an unhealed childhood. This offering must emanate from the most healed, present, and honest version of myself possible, imperfections aside. A profound shift occurred within my spirit as I stood at the precipice of preparation and release. It was not fear nor pressure, but a sacred readiness that emerged gradually, resonating rather than shouting.

When the time arrived for this offering to be released into the world, it transcended a fleeting moment into a ministry. It was not confined to a pulpit but met people where they were; in their headphones, bedrooms, and broken places, speaking directly to their souls.

As I dived deeper into my creative process, I felt a profound connection to the spirits of those who had come before me. The wounded little boy had once sung into the mirror, yearning for someone to see him. The teenager who had held onto so much emotion that it threatened to consume him and the young man who had married too early, loved too passionately, and nearly lost himself in the pursuit of being enough. They were all still present, but now, they served as witnesses to my journey of transformation. They observed my pain, but they also witnessed my growth.

They saw me rise from the ashes of my struggles, not despite them, but because of them.

In this sacred preparation, I found solace in the silence, the scarred pages, the lonely rehearsals, the late-night guitar sessions, the healing process, the heartbreak, and the long silence. These experiences, though challenging, were not punishments or delays. They were alignments, preparing me for the moment I would step onto that stage, wherever and whenever possible.

I am not waiting for perfection to emerge, but I am ready to embrace the truth. The world does not need another polished persona; it yearns for presence, authenticity, and offerings born from fire, faith, and a voice that refused to remain silent. Therefore, I continue to prepare, knowing that when I finally take that stage, my voice will resonate with the audience and carry the echoes of my struggles and the unwavering belief of those who have supported me.

This offering is not given for approval; it is a heartfelt expression of gratitude to life, God, and everyone who has remained steadfast. It is a thank-you to those who have guided me and those still searching for their way. What I am building now is not merely music; it is a movement, a testament to the resilience of the human spirit , and it all begins with a single, honest offering…a gift from the depths of my healing, given with my whole heart, wrapped in something that the world cannot manufacture presence.

Chapter 34

The Vision Beyond Me

"Your purpose is bigger than your healing-it's
the doorway for others to find theirs."

*A*s I continue my preparation, writing,

refining, and practicing journey, I have realized that
my music transcends my personal experiences.
Initially, it served as a mirror, reflecting my pain,
survival, and truth. However, I now perceive it as a
window, enabling others to glimpse their reflections.

I envision someone, perhaps an unknown
individual, reading my lyrics and resonating with the
sentiments expressed. I imagine someone who feels
marginalized finding solace in a melody I create
amidst the noise of everyday life. A stranger in a
crowded setting, overwhelmed by the world around
them, may suddenly feel less alone as a single line of
my song speaks to a hidden aspect of their emotions.

This realization dawns upon me: my music is no
longer solely about me. It has become a vehicle for
reaching out to those who remain silent, those who
bleed for love that will never be reciprocated, and
those unaware of the alternative perspectives to their
pain. This vision surpasses my capabilities and
extends beyond my healing. For when I rise from my
struggles, I possess the power to uplift others with
me. While I am not naïve, I acknowledge that music
alone cannot solve all problems. It cannot erase
trauma or rewrite the past. Nevertheless, it has a
profound impact: it reminds individuals that they are

not invisible, that they are not alone in their struggles, and that there is a glimmer of hope for survival. Perhaps this is the true purpose of my music, not merely for healing, but for demonstrating the possibility of healing.

When I was young and silent, I needed to be the voice I needed to offer the sound someone desperately seeks when they are on the brink of despair. When I envision the future beyond my current circumstances, I experience a profound sense of responsibility, not the burdening kind, but the kind that arises from love. It instills in me a sense of purpose that transcends fame and attention, emphasizing the profound impact my work can have. This vision sustains me through challenging days, when self-doubt creeps in and the creative process feels arduous. I question whether my efforts will ever resonate with the level of impact I aspire to achieve.

However, I remind myself that the significance lies not in my audience size but in the depth of the connections I foster. This realization fuels my determination to continue building my work, not for personal recognition. Still, it has the potential impact it can have on a single individual, a small group, or even a larger community. This vision transcends my existence; it begins with my unwavering commitment to the calling, the process, and my aspiration to transcend the limitations of survival. I envision myself becoming a beacon of hope for those who have endured pain, reminding them that life exists beyond their struggles. When my work finally reaches its intended recipients, it will no longer feel like mine; it will belong to them, embodying the essence of true purpose, the transformative power of multiplication.

As I embrace this path, I realize that my voice is not the sole determinant of my impact. The essence flows through it; the melodies, the lyrics, and the moments of vulnerability that once held immense personal significance. These elements have transcended their original purpose of expression and now serve as conduits for divine transmission. They carry something transcendent that was never meant to remain confined within my limitations.

I contemplate the countless individuals who may never meet me, including the young child struggling to comprehend why those entrusted with their protection made them feel unlovable. I envision the single parent, barely holding on, finding solace in headphones and a song that offers solace, assuring them that their feelings of brokenness are not irrational. And I imagine the soul, exhausted after a long shift, gazing into the void until a melody pierces through the silence, illuminating the darkness like light through smoke.

If even a single soul feels seen and less alone through my work, then every ache I have endured becomes worthwhile. I gained a profound understanding at this juncture: my narrative has transcended its ownership and become a conduit for divine grace. It has the potential to serve as a soundtrack for individuals grappling with survival challenges, providing solace and inspiration amid adversity.

Previously, I believed that success was solely measured by numerical indicators such as streams, followers, chart positions, and applause. However, I have come to recognize that true success lies in my music's profound impact on individuals, evoking moments of respite and solace. My music resonates with people, and this resonance cannot be faked; it is a result of living authentically and embracing one's true self.

This vision extends beyond my personal experiences, as I am merely the messenger, the instrument, and the open channel through which the divine energy flows. However, the essence of God…its spirit, source, and authentic presence, effectuates the healing process. All I had to do was consent to allowing this transformative energy to pass through me, even when I felt unprepared or vulnerable.

I now comprehend that healing is contagious, spreading spontaneously and silently, reaching unexpected destinations. This upcoming chapter involves embracing the transformative power of my past struggles and experiences, allowing them to become the foundation of my connection with others. It consists of transcending my limitations and envisioning a future that surpasses my current perception.

Furthermore, I trust that my journey has not been in vain. The nights of silent tears, the moments of despair, and the prayers whispered with trembling hands have not gone unnoticed. They have served a purpose, preparing me for survival and the role of a guiding light for others. I reflect on the moments when I nearly succumbed to silence, questioning the relevance of my music and succumbing to the allure of doubt. I recall the heartbreaks that threatened to extinguish my spirit. Yet, I resisted these temptations, recognizing that silence would not serve anyone.

Shame only holds power when concealed. Therefore, I chose to speak despite my trembling voice, imperfect narrative, and fear. For somewhere, someone is yearning for a genuine connection.

This is where the vision becomes a legacy, not the kind etched in stone but quietly inscribed in another's survival narrative. The kind that conveys: *"I encountered this song during my darkest hour and found solace in its melody."*

"This lyric allowed me to confront and express emotions I had suppressed for years."

"I believed I was alone in experiencing this feeling until I heard your voice."

That is legacy, not applause or fame, but impact. And here is what I firmly believe in every fiber of my being: The story we conceal the most often resonates with someone in need. We become mirrors, invitations, and permission sources when we cease concealing it. This proves that scars can be aesthetically pleasing, pain can be transformed, and music can be a healing balm. Consequently, whenever I compose a song or sing from that raw, sacred place within me, I remind myself that this is no longer about those who abandoned me, attempted to silence me, or doubted my abilities. It is about those who are currently listening and seeking solace. Perhaps, just perhaps, my voice can provide that solace.

This sustains me, not ego or ambition, but the realization that this vision transcends my limitations. I am merely embarking on this journey. Previously, I believed I needed complete healing before offering assistance. However, I now comprehend that hope is found in the process, not completion. It is not about perfection; it is about presence. Present your story, share your pain, and be vulnerable enough to convey, *"I am still evolving, still rising. You can, too."*

This vision beyond my reach is not a spotlight but a lantern. A steadfast light in the darkness that proclaims, "There is a path here. Proceed." I now bear this light, not because I possess all the answers, but because I have experienced the void of walking without one. I refuse to allow others to remain in the darkness if my flame can guide them forward.

While I may never encounter anyone who hears my music or comprehends the full extent of this calling, I am not burdened by such concerns. Impact does not seek recognition; it merely demands courage, and I now possess that attribute. Therefore, I persist in my presence, creative endeavors, and journey toward the vision that chose me long before I comprehended its significance. Each lyric I compose, each truth I impart, and each scar I reveal with grace conveys a singular message:

You are not beyond repair to become a blessing. You are not too late to embark on a new chapter. And your voice...yes, your voice still possesses power.

The vision beyond me transcends my ownership; it is destined to awaken something within the hearts of others, enabling them to experience it as well. Together, we serve as evidence that pain can have a birth purpose. Silence can yield to song; no narrative is too disheveled to hold significance. I was not merely created for the purpose of singing; I was also destined to remind, heal, construct, dream, and guide others toward their own destinies. As I venture into the unknown, I approach it with open hands, heart, and eyes. For now, I have finally grasped the truth: The vision was never solely about me; it was always about the potential for growth and transformation that I embody. And its journey has only just commenced.

Chapter 35
When the Time Comes
*"What's meant for you will never miss you—
but you still have to be ready when it
arrives."*

$\mathscr{E}$ach day now presents a delicate equilibrium between preparation and patience. I am constructing an intangible yet palpable entity, akin to standing amidst a sunrise, anticipating the light's arrival even before it touches the horizon. There are moments when I am consumed by the question of when the moment will arrive, when the stage will be prepared, and when the doors will finally open. However, I am reminded that rushing the present is counterproductive. Instead, I focus on becoming the individual prepared for the moment's arrival. While I cannot control the timing or force the right individuals to hear my music, I can control my preparation. I have honed my craft, remained steadfast in my purpose, and maintained an open heart even during the waiting period. When the time finally comes, I am certain it will. I aspire to be ready musically, spiritually, emotionally, and energetically. I aspire to step into that moment with clarity, fully comprehending my identity and purpose.

Occasionally, I envision the initial performance on a larger stage. The lights, the hushed murmur of the audience, and the moment just before the commencement of the performance do not evoke a sense of performance for me. Instead, I perceive them as a meeting, a convergence of my narrative and theirs. It is a moment when all the experiences, struggles, and preparations I have endured will finally resonate with someone who requires them. I am certain that this moment is not arbitrary; it is divinely aligned and will occur precisely when it is destined to, not a moment too early or too late. Therefore, I continue my preparation, pouring my heart into my lyrics and melodies, living in a manner that honors my purpose even before its complete manifestation. Faith is not about stagnation; it is about diligently working while awaiting the fulfillment of one's aspirations. I believe there is a purpose for this season of preparation, it is shaping me and teaching me patience. By cultivating resilience, I am prepared to confidently step onto the stage, fully immersed and anchored within it.

My aspiration extends beyond mere singing; I envision myself as a transformative presence, inspiring others to recognize their inherent strength. I aspire to create a space for healing, not just with a microphone, but with a profound sense of purpose. I patiently await my moment, but my anticipation is not idle. It is guided by faith, preparation, and a quiet confidence that my destiny will find me. When it does, I will be fully prepared. There is a sacredness in becoming ready in the realm of the unseen. Applause and validation may not be present, but the work and the silent encouragement to persevere suffice. I have learned that external confirmation is unnecessary to fulfill one's calling. The essence lies in consistent action and unwavering commitment.

Previously, I envisioned the "moment" arriving with grandeur, a dramatic shift, a viral sensation, or an overnight affirmation. However, I now recognize that this moment may unfold more gradually, similar

252

to the slow dawn. It is not always immediately apparent when the light breaks through, but one looks up and perceives its presence. Therefore, I diligently attend quiet rehearsals, daily disciplines, and unseen hours. These moments are where proper alignment is forged, integrity is built, and ego diminishes while purpose flourishes. During these moments, I learn to carry my gift not for external praise, but with a sense of presence. I have repeatedly contemplated that my vision may not materialize as anticipated. However, the consistent response is simple: something superior will emerge. When one's intentions are pure, their mission is love, and their offering is genuine, it becomes impossible to miss one's destined path. Therefore, I have ceased chasing the stage; I am diligently preparing for it. I live as if it is already mine, not out of arrogance but from a profound sense of alignment. If the stage takes time to manifest, I am prepared to await its arrival patiently. When it does, I will not merely step onto it but fully embrace and embody my purpose. I am already prepared for this journey. Previously, I believed the ultimate rewards would be recognition, applause, and the industry's validation. However, I now comprehend that the valid reward lies within myself, the emotional maturity to handle praise and silence, the spiritual clarity to remain grounded regardless of the platform's height, and the self-trust that assures me of my worth even when no one claps. This is the work fame cannot provide; it is the strength that arises from standing in truth, even when no one is watching.

A quiet form of preparation, often overlooked, is sacred. It lies behind the lyrics, the conversations with God that shape the melody, and the nights spent repeatedly rewriting the same verse, not for external validation, but because my soul demands deeper exploration. This season has been a period of refinement, a holy pause that has not hindered me but built me up. For what awaits me requires more than talent; it demands wholeness. Therefore, I honor the waiting, the pace, and the days when inspiration eludes me. Even in these moments, something is still being stirred.

My preparation is not merely a means of securing entry but a foundation that will anchor me once I am inside. There will come a moment, perhaps quiet or perhaps loud, when all my preparation culminates in its moment. This will not feel like a surprise; it will feel like alignment. For I have not waited idly; I have waited with intention. I have planted the seeds, nurtured the ground, and consistently responded to my calling, even when it remained invisible to others.

When the time arrives, it will not merely be a performance but a homecoming, a return to the purpose that has always resonated with my soul. As I step onto that stage, whatever form it may take, I will embody the strength and authenticity cultivated through this sacred preparation. I will not seek approval for my performance. Instead, I will offer something sacred. Not merely a voice, but a vessel. It is a song and a mirror, allowing others to perceive their light through mine.

During my waiting period, I gained valuable insights: genuine transformation cannot be hastened, and profound transformations occur when no one observes. And I will not merely be discovered when the opportune moment arrives. I will be delivered into the purpose that has always been my destiny.

Therefore, I persist in my dedication to my work, silence, and sacred preparation. For when that moment finally arrives, I will not be unprepared. I will be ready.

Chapter 36
The Closing Note

"The story isn't over. It's just changing hands, becoming something bigger than me."

*R*eflecting on the shared experiences, memories, and resilience that have shaped my journey, I realize that this book transcends a conventional narrative of an ending. Instead, it embodies the transformative process of becoming.

I have endured periods of immense pain that felt insurmountable, traversing seasons of betrayal, rejection, and loneliness that profoundly impacted my growth. I faced the lack of support from those who should have stood by me, finding solace and belonging in those who chose to embrace me. Despite these setbacks, I have experienced both falls and rises, and my journey continues to unfold.

This narrative does not conclude with a neatly tied bow. There are still fragments of healing, dreams in progress, and music within me yearning to connect with the world. However, I have realized that none of these experiences was in vain. Each heartbreak became a poignant lyric, each silence a verse, and each moment of perceived finality nurtured the seeds of new beginnings. Consequently, what once felt like pain has metamorphosed into a purposeful journey.

The precise destination of this path remains uncertain, but I am sure it leads to a realm of beauty. For I have learned that embracing one's truth unveils the unfolding path, even if the entirety of the journey remains veiled. This is a lesson I impart to the reader: your story holds significance, your scars do not diminish your worth, and your survival is not the culmination of your existence; instead, it marks the commencement of your purposeful contributions.

I am currently constructing my stage, refining my music, and embodying the role of the messenger destined to share my message. However, I anticipate the moment when these words, these songs, and this journey will resonate with those who require them most. At that juncture, they will transcend my ownership and become a shared experience for you, for anyone who has grappled with the weight of their own life.

Therefore, this is not a farewell; it is an invitation to persevere, to trust in the timing of your journey, and to believe that the trials you have endured can transcend their pain and manifest into something greater. The narrative continues to unfold on the stage I am building, in the lyrics I am crafting, and in the connections that await. As music finally enters the world, it transcends mere songs, becoming a profound reminder that healing exists, purpose awaits, and solitude is an illusion.

This is merely the beginning, and I eagerly anticipate our reunion beyond the melody. If you have persevered through this journey, you have not simply read my story but embraced it. You have endured the trials with me, stood in the silence, faced the storms, and resonated with the songs. In the process, perhaps you have glimpsed your reflection, a testament to the essence of this narrative. It was never merely a book or a collection of memories; it was a mirror, a bridge, and an extended hand in the darkness.

There were moments when I contemplated abandoning this writing, not because I doubted the words' validity, but because I hesitated to release them to the world. I feared exposing vulnerable aspects of myself, transforming my pain into public view, and trusting that someone, somewhere, would comprehend. However, I now recognize that this story was never solely mine; it was destined to be shared. Perhaps you have felt marginalized, burdened by wounds others could not perceive. Maybe you have yearned for someone to acknowledge your experiences. Allow this final chapter to serve as that moment, providing a gentle landing for your heart. It offers permission to recognize your pain without succumbing to it, transforming it into something meaningful.

I am unaware of your challenges and the silence you have endured, but I firmly believe you remain present. This presence holds significance; it signifies that your story is not concluded, your voice remains potent, and you possess a sacred offering to the world, even as you grapple with its nature.

As I conclude this book, not as a definitive end, but as a symbolic transfer of the torch, I leave you with these profound truths: you are not broken; you are evolving. You are not lost; you are in the process of discovery. You are not alone; you are perceived, felt, and cherished. The song continues, and I encourage you to write your verse, sing your melody, and live your truth authentically. I will be listening and cheering you on, and I will be present in every lyric, every silence, and every echo of your transformation.

As I delve deeper into this journey, I realize that this is not merely about storytelling but about transmission. Every word I have written is a piece of energy released into the world; an offering of truth wrapped in vulnerability. While my story is deeply personal, it no longer feels private. Because the pain that has been healed has become wisdom, and wisdom, when shared, becomes light. I once believed that fame and public recognition were necessary for my life to have meaning, that healing required a grand stage. However, I now understand that the most transformative moments occur in the quiet.

In the spaces between verses, in the glances shared when one person's truth allows another to own theirs, and if this book, this voice, and this offering have touched even one heart, it has fulfilled its purpose. I recall the nights when I cried into songs that no one had heard, the moments when I sat at my desk questioning the value of my efforts, and the days when I walked into work exhausted from carrying a dream that seemed too heavy for others to perceive. Now, I comprehend that those were sacred moments as well. The waiting, the struggle, and the quiet preparation were all sacred. Because every second, every moment, was leading me to this point. To the threshold of something greater, to the final breath of one chapter and the exhalation that heralds the beginning of another. As I sit here closing this book, I do not feel like I am bidding farewell; I feel like I am sending something off.

Like a message in a bottle, propelled into another's heart, I hope it finds them when they need it most. Once a personal narrative, it belongs to the hearts it was destined to touch. It transcends its original purpose as a chronicle of survival, becoming a living, breathing testament to the transformative power of even the deepest pain. If you hold this book, you witness that wounds do not diminish one's worth; they shape their purpose. Healing is an arduous, unpredictable journey, yet it remains beautiful. Abandoning what has broken us is not a sign of weakness but a manifestation of strength in motion.

I did not compose this work to seek praise; instead, I sought to evoke a profound emotional response, to be remembered, and to endure in the quiet corners of the human experience, the late nights, the concealed tears, and the whispered prayers of those who believe their solitude is unobserved. You are not invisible; you remain present. Consequently, your narrative is far from concluded.

This chapter concludes, but the melody persists. It will be incorporated into the music I eventually release, the voice I now honor, and the lives of those, like mine, who are learning to rise from the ashes and sing. When that moment arrives, when my voice finally reaches the ears and hearts it was meant for, it will transcend mere sound; it will become a legacy.

Let this serve as the concluding note: not an ending but a spark, not a period but a hand reaching out to invite you to join me. Healing possesses a sound, and you have just heard it.

Epilogue

"The End Was Never the End"

For an extended period, I believed that survival was the sole objective. If I could endure the excruciating pain, withstand the oppressive silence, and transcend the pervasive shame, perhaps that would suffice. However, the healing process unveiled a profound truth: survival is merely a component of a broader journey transformative to the process of becoming the authentic version of oneself, free from the world's attempts to shatter one's spirit. This book is not a plea for pity but a declaration of my resilience in the face of adversity. It is a testament to my ability to find beauty amidst the ashes and to choose love even in the face of its failures. Moreover, it is a profound revelation that I have learned to release the shackles of approval-seeking and the desperate need for recognition. I have released myself from the toxic relationships with individuals who consistently misunderstood me and chose to remain small to maintain a semblance of peace. Letting go did not imply forgetting; instead, it liberated me. Three years have elapsed since the commencement of my rebuilding journey. I now comprehend that the most courageous act I ever undertook was to cease waiting for external validation and instead embrace self-selection. While challenging days still present themselves, there are moments when the echoes of the past resound with greater intensity than I would prefer. However, I have developed the strength to respond, to move forward, and to transform the places where I once shed tears into spaces of joy and expression. The narrative does not conclude here; it serves as the opening chapter of a transformative journey. From this point forward, my existence is not driven by the need to prove anything; instead, I channel my energy into fulfilling the purpose that guided my birth, the pursuit of music, the dissemination of a message, the presence of a stage, and the potential for love. If you have read these pages and encountered a reflection of your journey, know that you are not lagging, you are not shattered, and that you are not too late. You are embarking on a transformative path of self-discovery and growth. Just as I am, and when you hear my voice resonate through a song, stage, or stadium, remember that it carries fragments of our experiences. For healing may commence alone, but it does not culminate in isolation. We rise together, and I eagerly anticipate connecting with you on this transformative journey.

See you soon,
Mark

For The Ones Who Stayed

To those who saw me when I felt invisible,
Who chose me, stood by me, and reminded me
that love is presence, not perfection.
This story carries your fingerprints in every
chapter.
You were the light when I forgot how to see.
You were the reason I kept going.
Thank you for being part of my healing.
This is as much yours as it is mine.

Dear Future Me,

You've come a long way, my friend. You've
overcome challenges and found strength within
yourself, even without the people you once thought
were essential. You've learned to breathe
independently, walk away from pain, and love
yourself in the quiet moments. You've carried the
world's weight on your shoulders, yet you've
shown up with a heart full of courage. You've
stopped waiting for permission and stopped
begging to be chosen. Amid all that pain, you've
discovered your power and become your answer.

So, if you ever find yourself lost or unsure of
who you are, remember this: you didn't come this
far to shrink or blend in. You were never meant to
be quiet about your story.

You are proof of your strength, your purpose,
and your resilience. You are still rising and have
the power to make a difference.

Go forth and take up space. Speak your truth.
And never apologize for surviving like this.
You've got this, my friend.

Love,
-Me

What This Book Awakened in Me

This space is yours.
Take a deep breath and let yourself feel what you're feeling. If you're ready, let it all out.
This page is for you to write down what this story stirred up inside you. What memories came to mind? What did you release? What are you ready to reclaim?
Your words matter, too.
Whether it's a letter to your younger self, a message to the person you're becoming, or just a few thoughts scribbled down while you're healing and hopeful.
Be honest. Be yourself.

A Message to the Ones Still Holding on

If you're feeling overwhelmed, teary-eyed, or like your story doesn't matter anymore, this is for you. I don't know your whole story, but I know what it's like to wonder if your struggles still matter. I know what it's like to hold on by a thread, smiling to hide your pain, shrinking your voice to avoid questions, and wondering if the pain you carry makes you too much or not enough. But hear me: You're not too far gone. You're not beyond repair. You're not alone in this. You're still here, and that means your story isn't over. You don't have to have everything figured out. You don't have to be healed to be worthy. You must keep breathing, choosing, and reaching, even if it's messy or slow. I wrote this book for you. For the one still standing in the fire, unsure if the flames will ever die down. For the one who keeps waking up even when life keeps knocking them down. For the one who needed someone to say "Me too. And I made it through." You will rise. Not because the pain disappears overnight, but because there's power in not giving up. And when you're ready, you'll tell your story too, and it will be someone else's lifeline. Until then, take this page with you as a reminder. As a whisper. As proof that someone who once felt what you feel now made it through and is still cheering for you on the other side.

— Mark Chachere

What's next

This book represents the initial chapter of a larger narrative. The subsequent musical compositions serve as a continuation of the healing process.

However, another story awaits—a narrative that emerged during the contemplative moments between chapters. I am currently engaged in the creative process of developing a fictional series that chronicles the journey of a mysterious soul named Kai. This wanderer traverses the boundaries between realms of light and shadow, burdened with gifts he did not seek and truths that the world is not yet prepared to acknowledge. Kai's narrative transcends mere fiction; it resonates with the emotional echoes of every individual who has ever felt different, destined, and profoundly misunderstood. Through Kai's journey, I explore identity, energy, spiritual awakening, chosen purpose, and the quiet fortitude that emerges from solitude. As the pages of Kai's world begin to take shape, so does the melody of my music.

My musical compositions embody the same essence rhythm of survival, love, and transformation. The future trajectory of this creative endeavor remains uncertain. Nevertheless, I am sure that it will be authentic. I invite you to accompany me as I blend truth and artistry.

About the author

Mark Chachere Jr., a storyteller, truth-teller, and a soul on a mission. He was born into adversity and refined through faith. His life has been a journey of rising from the places that sought to extinguish his spirit. As a songwriter and survivor, he transforms pain into purpose, crafting narratives and music that resonate with the voices of those who have felt unseen, unchosen, or unloved.

His memoir, "The Strength in Letting Go," transcends a mere recounting of the past; it is a reclamation of his journey. This raw, honest, healing narrative traverse's trauma, estrangement, chosen family, and the arduous path back to self-worth.

When not weaving words into powerful narratives, Mark creates music rooted in emotional truth, songs that penetrate the depths of individuals' lives, offering solace and reminding them of their solitude. Every lyric, every page, and every post is an offering: a testament to the transformative power of brokenness and the sacredness of survival.

This is not a farewell; it is an anticipation of a reunion. When that day arrives, it will transcend the confines of these pages. It will resonate in a song that carries your story as profoundly as it carries mine…echoing from a stage, a screen, or a stadium somewhere near you. I did not merely survive; I embarked on a journey of growth and fulfillment.

Acknowledgments

To God, my anchor, my healer, and the reason I'm
still standing. Thank you for walking with me
through the valleys, whispering purpose into my
pain, and never letting go of me, even when I let go
of myself. My chosen family Mike, Tiffany, Zach,
Tom, Tommy, Eva, Lora, Bret, and every soul who
became a safe place when I had nowhere else to
run. You didn't just show up. You stayed. You saw
me in my rawest moments and loved me anyway.
You are proof that blood is not the only thing that
defines family, presence does. To the ones who
called me "Uncle," they wrapped their arms around
me and made me feel like I belonged, thank you for
giving me moments of joy and innocence I never
thought I'd experience. You healed parts of me
without even knowing it. To the ones who broke
me, thank you, too. You taught me what love is
not. You taught me how to fight for myself. And
through every betrayal, silence, and scar, you gave
me the material for transformation. I turned what
tried to destroy me into something divine. To every
reader holding this book: thank you for meeting me
here. In these pages. In these wounds. In this truth.
You may not know me personally, but if you've
ever felt invisible, discarded, or like the world
didn't make space for you, this was written with
you in mind. I see you. I am you and I promise
you; healing is real.

To my future, music, my future love, my little
family still in the making, I'm ready for you. This
book is the closure. What comes next is the

miracle. And to the Almighty, my steadfast anchor, my source of solace, and the reason I endure, I express my profound gratitude for your unwavering presence throughout my journey. Your guidance through the darkest valleys, your whispered encouragement amidst my suffering, and your unshakable support even when I faltered and lost sight of myself are all deeply appreciated.

To the young boy I once was, who struggled under the weight of pain, I have kept my promise. We have emerged victoriously, transforming our suffering into strength. You are no longer confined to the shadows but free to soar. You're free.

www.ingramcontent.com/pod-product-compliance
Lightning Source LLC
Chambersburg PA
CBHW021709120626
46545CB00004B/1479